The Paddler's Journal & Companion

DOUBLEDAY CANADA LIMITED / RUSSET BOOKS

Copyright © 1997 Peter Maher, Laurie Coulter
and Paula Chabanais

All rights reserved. No part of this publication may be
reproduced, stored in a retrieval system, or transmitted,
in any form or by any means, electronic, mechanical,
photocopying, recording or otherwise, without the prior
written permission of Doubleday Canada Limited.

Canadian Cataloguing in Publication Data

Maher, Peter, 1941-

The paddler's journal & companion

ISBN 0-385-25668-X
1. Canoes and canoeing I. Coulter, Laurie, 1951-
II. Chabanais, Paula. III. Title. IV. Title: The paddler's
journal and companion.

GV783.M33 1997   797.1'22   C96-932597-5

Cover and text design: Peter Maher
Case photograph: Arthur Herriott
Copy editing: Alison Reid
Printed and bound in Canada

Note: The first-aid prevention and treatment
information contained in this book is not intended to be
substituted for consultation with your physician. All
matters pertaining to your health should be directed to a
health care professional.

Packaged by
Russet Books
Division of Paula Chabanais & Associates Limited
372 Sackville Street
Toronto, Ontario
M4X 1S5

Published in Canada by
Doubleday Canada Limited
105 Bond Street
Toronto, Ontario
M5B 1Y3

Acknowledgments
The authors would like to thank the many friends and
colleagues who gave their encouragement and support, in
particular Erich Volk, Bill Thomas and the "Voyageurs"
Alan Daniel, Paul Caulfield, Arthur Herriott, Jim
McConnell and Jon McKee.

"Baptism" from *Mid-River* by Dale Zieroth (Toronto: The
House of Anansi Press, 1981). Reprinted by permission of
Stoddart Publishing Co. Limited, Don Mills, Ont.

Illustration credits: *Adventures in the Wilderness* (William
Murray), cover, 5, 27, 75; Metropolitan Toronto Reference
Library, 2, 8, 11, 15, 18, 21, 22, 29, 33, 46, 51, 53, 57, 59,
79, 84; Public Archives of Canada, 55; *A Thousand Miles
in the Rob Roy Canoe on Twenty Rivers and Lakes of
Europe* (John MacGregor), 3. Illustrations on pages 54,
62, 63, 68, 69, 72, 73 and 77 by Jason Maher.

If you have any suggestions for additions to future
editions, please contact Russet Books.

*In mid-river we join the ancient force
of mud and leaves moving in their journey
down the face of the continent and
after the first dance of leaving
one element for another, we fall quiet,
waiting for the silence to give us a
glimpse of history.*

from "Baptism" by Dale Zieroth, 1981

voyageur

1 *Fur Trade, Hist.* a. one of the canoemen or boatmen, usually a French Canadian, Orkneyman, Indian, or Métis, who crewed the vessels of the inland fur trade.
b. any of those journeying into the wilderness of the Northwest, both engaged servants and company officers.
2 *Hist.* a boatman on the St. Lawrence River and tributary waters.
3 *Hist.* a soldier in the Voyageur Corps.
4 **a.** a person who travels the northern wilderness as trapper, canoeman, dog-driver, etc.; an experienced woodsman.
b. any traveller of the rivers and trails of the wilderness, especially by canoe.

A Concise Dictionary of Canadianisms

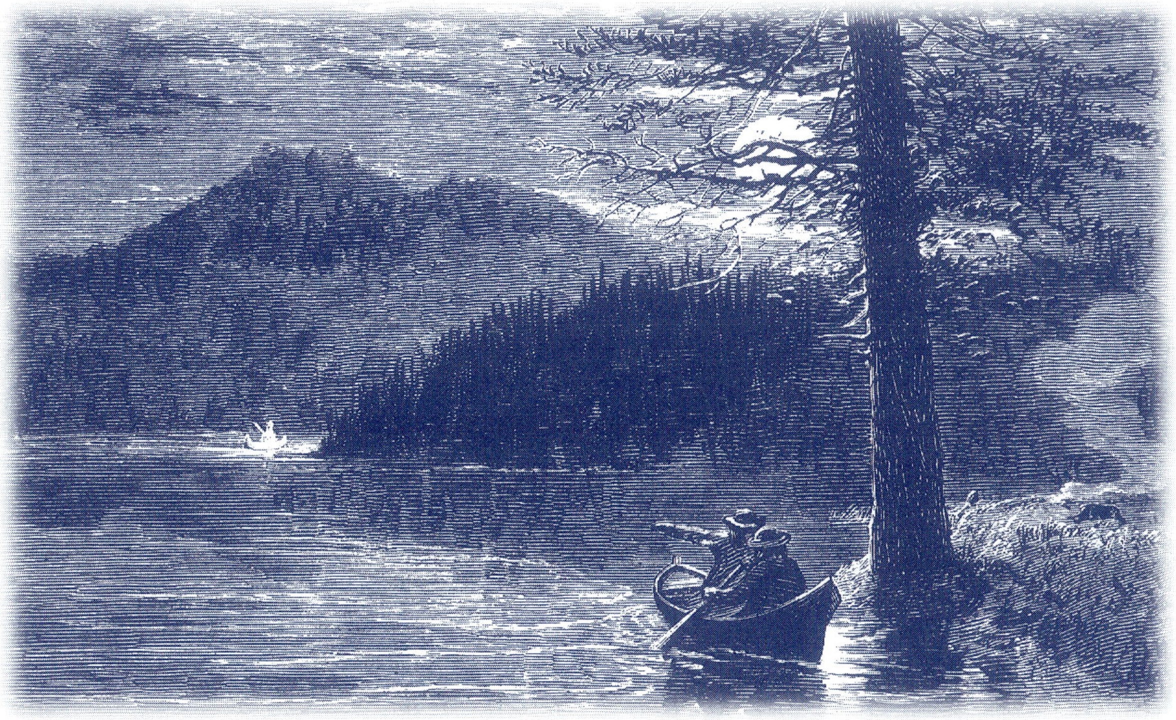

Contents

The largest canoes are 32 feet in length, 5 1/2 in breadth and 2 1/2 in depth. They are borne across the longest portages by two men... and although their materials are so slight, they will carry 3200 lb. each, besides the crew. A loaded canoe has six paddlers, two of whom sit upon each bench, the foreman being single and the steersman standing in the stern with a long paddle. A lightly loaded canoe can stow conveniently ten paddlers and is capable of going seven miles an hour for a whole day.

Robert Hood, *To the Arctic by Canoe 1819-1821: The Journal and Paintings of Robert Hood, Midshipman with Franklin*

TRIP PLANNER
Menu suggestions / 9
Menu planner / 12
Food checklist / 14
Camp kitchen checklist / 16
Camping gear checklist / 20
First-aid kit checklist / 22
Photography gear checklist / 24
Tackle checklist / 26

CANOEING CHECKLISTS
Equipment / 28
Personal gear / 30

KAYAKING CHECKLISTS
Equipment / 34
Personal gear / 36

CAMPSITE LORE
Camp stoves and wood fires / 40
Songs, tales and customs / 42
Blackflies, little blackflies ... / 52
Knots / 54
Rubaboo and bannockburn / 56
Carry in, carry out / 58

THE SKY
Weather forecasting / 60
Star charts / 62

Flora and Fauna
Bears, leeches, snakes and jellyfish / 64
Animal tracks / 68
Animal sightings / 70
Bird silhouettes / 72
Bird sightings / 74
Plants to avoid along the way / 76

Fishing
Cooking the catch / 78
Record of fish caught / 80

Emergencies
Basic first aid and injury prevention / 82
Signaling in an emergency / 84

Bibliography / 86

Trip Journal / 89

First Portage on the Little River, John Woolford, 1821

Menu suggestions

Potatoes, boiled, fried, or mashed
Venison, roast
Venison steak, broiled, fried
Venison sausages, hash, spitted
Lake trout (salmon), boiled, baked, broiled, chowder
Trout (spotted), fried, broiled, spitted
Pancakes, with maple sirup
Bread, warm and stale, both
Coffee
Tea

William H. H. Murray's menu for his trips to the Adirondacks in the 1860s, from *Adventures in the Wilderness,* 1869

Good food can make the difference between an enjoyable trip and a disappointing one. The planning of the menu must take into account the people involved and the level of effort required. Younger people, for example, eat larger quantities and can metabolize food more quickly than older or heavier people. The timing of the trip must also be considered, because the body burns more energy on cool days than on warm.

A person taking part in outdoor activities needs roughly between 3,000 to 4,500 calories per day compared with a voyageur's nearly 7,000 calories. But then most of us don't paddle eighty miles in sixteen-hour stretches beginning at 3:00 a.m. — "57,600 strokes with the paddle," as reported by Thomas McKenney in 1826. Carbohydrates should make up 65 percent of a wilderness diet, fats 25 percent and protein 10 percent. On the following pages are some menu suggestions for modern-day voyageurs.

BREAKFAST

Fresh fruit (oranges, apples, wild
  berries)

Fresh eggs (early in trip)

Dried eggs (later in trip)

Peameal bacon (early in trip)

Rye bread (early in trip)

Bagels (early in trip)

Bannock (later in trip)

Pancakes

Granola

Oatmeal

Muffins

LUNCH

Peanut butter and jam

Bread

Pita bread

Crackers

Dried soup (on layover days)

Cheese

Smoked meat

Dried fruit

Trail mix

DINNER

Bread

Dried soup

Fresh meat and vegetables (first day)

Meat stew (prefrozen at home before
  departure)

Fresh fish

Couscous

Pasta

Chili

Vegetable curry

Potato dishes

Lentil and bean dishes

Rice dishes

Dried vegetables

Desserts

Fresh fruit

Instant puddings/cakes

Dried fruit

Fruit compote

Rice pudding

Cookies

Snacks

Trail mix

Dried fruit

Nuts

Granola bars

Chocolate

Drinks

Coffee

Tea

Powdered milk

Fruit drink mix

Hot chocolate

Bacon, 7 lb
Butter, 4 lb
Chipped beef, 1/2 lb
Tea, 1 lb
Klim, 2 pound cans
G. Washington coffee, 1 can
Evaporated milk, 6 small cans
Prunes, 3 lb
Sugar, 4 lb
Beans, 2 lb
Onions, 12 large Spanish
Jam, Strawberry, 1 lb
Cheese, 1 lb
Pancake flour, 4 packages
Oranges, 6
Chocolate bars, 7 ten-cent ones
Salt, 1 lb
Bread, 9 loaves
Rolled oats, 6 lb

John D. Robins and a companion's food list for a sixteen-day trip to Algonquin Park in the 1930s, supplemented with fish, from *The Incomplete Anglers*

Menu planner

Date of trip:

Day	Breakfast	Lunch	Dinner	Snack

We had our usual breakfast of granola with powdered milk and sugar covered with hot water. Our beverage in the morning was hot chocolate. We had no coffee along and only drank tea in the evening because it had a diuretic effect. Don had no problem with that. He had a bailing can that doubled as a pee can. For me it was a whole lot different. My kidneys behaved. I managed twelve-hour stretches with no problem, except twice. Once I had to step out onto a reef covered by six inches of water and the other time I just wet my pants.

Victoria Jason, Kabloona in the Yellow Kayak: One Woman's Journey Through the Northwest Passage, 1995

Date of trip:

Day	Breakfast	Lunch	Dinner	Snack

Food checklist

Number	Item	Date	Date	Date	Date	Date
....	....	....	....	....	....	....
○	○	○	○	○		
○	○	○	○	○		
○	○	○	○	○		
○	○	○	○	○		
○	○	○	○	○		
○	○	○	○	○		
○	○	○	○	○		
○	○	○	○	○		
○	○	○	○	○		
○	○	○	○	○		
○	○	○	○	○		
○	○	○	○	○		
○	○	○	○	○		
○	○	○	○	○		
○	○	○	○	○		
○	○	○	○	○		
○	○	○	○	○		
○	○	○	○	○		

The first nation that we came to was that of the Folle Avoine ... The wild oat, whose name they bear because it is found in their country, is a sort of grass ... In the month of September ... they go in canoes through these fields of wild oats; they shake its ears into the canoe, on both sides, as they pass through. The grain falls out easily, if it be ripe, and they obtain their supply in a short time. But, in order to clean it from the straw and to remove it from a husk in which it is enclosed, they dry it in the smoke, upon a wooden grating, under which they maintain a slow fire for some days. When the oats are thoroughly dry, they put them in a skin made into a bag, thrust it into a hole dug in the ground for this purpose, and tread it with their feet — so long and so vigorously that the grain separates from the straw, and is very easily winnowed. After this, they pound it to reduce it to flour, or even, without pounding it, they boil it in water, and season it with fat.

Louis Jolliet and Jacques Marquette, *The Mississippi Voyage of Jolliet and Marquette, 1673*

Camping Out (detail), Alice Killaly, c.1867

Number	Item	Date	Date	Date	Date	Date ....
		○	○	○	○	○
		○	○	○	○	○
		○	○	○	○	○
		○	○	○	○	○
		○	○	○	○	○
		○	○	○	○	○
		○	○	○	○	○
		○	○	○	○	○
		○	○	○	○	○
		○	○	○	○	○
		○	○	○	○	○
		○	○	○	○	○
		○	○	○	○	○
		○	○	○	○	○
		○	○	○	○	○
		○	○	○	○	○
		○	○	○	○	○

Camp kitchen checklist

After the first day we had read all the old Newsweeks that Ray had given us in case we got stranded. The second day we read the ads. By the third day we were reading the parts of the magazine that no one should be forced to read.... It was not that we didn't have other things to do. When we didn't want to read anymore we could always go down to the canoe and sort and count the food. Of course, sleeping was always an option, as was sorting through the food. Did I mention that? We were beginning to learn French. On each box of Canadian pancake mix we found our lesson. It was the perfect time for a perfect family breakfast. L'ideal pour un parfait petit déjeuner en famille.

American canoeist Scott Anderson, stranded on the shores of Lake Winnipeg during a 1987 trip from Lake Superior to York Factory, from his book *Distant Fires*, 1990

	Date	Date	Date	Date	Date
	....	....	....	....	....
EQUIPMENT					
Camp stove	O	O	O	O	O
Fuel	O	O	O	O	O
Grill for wood fire	O	O	O	O	O
Saw or ax	O	O	O	O	O
Matches, stashed throughout gear in waterproof containers	O	O	O	O	O
Lighter	O	O	O	O	O
Candles	O	O	O	O	O
Reflector oven or baking device	O	O	O	O	O
Nesting set of pots and bag	O	O	O	O	O
Frying pan	O	O	O	O	O
Plate, bowl, mug per person	O	O	O	O	O
Knife, fork, spoon per person	O	O	O	O	O

In the old days of canoe tripping at Camp Pathfinder in Algonquin Park, we always carried a cast iron frying pan. Although heavy, it had several advantages: it wouldn't get bent out of shape when someone stepped on or dropped a pack, the outside didn't have to be soaped up prior to use on a wood fire, and (best of all) it provided after-dinner entertainment. It worked like this.

After dinner, the pan was turned upside down on the fire to burn out whatever crud may have accumulated upon the inner surface. When the frying pan was nearly red hot, a staff member would wrap the handle with a bandana, pick it up, and run screaming toward the lake where the pan would be dropped hastily into the water, generating clouds of steam, and rounds of applause. While showy, this was effective, because by the time the pan cooled off, a quick wipe with a scouring pad would get it clean.

The ritual was not without drawbacks, however. I watched one night as the trip leader ran screaming toward the lake, flipped the frying pan into the water, and saw it skip across the surface like a stone — three times — before sinking into the depths.

Bill Thomas, a native of Rochester who still returns to Algonquin Park each year to canoe

	Date	Date	Date	Date	Date
Spatula	○	○	○	○	○
Kitchen knife	○	○	○	○	○
Serving spoon	○	○	○	○	○
Tongs	○	○	○	○	○
Welder's gloves or pot holder	○	○	○	○	○
Aluminum foil	○	○	○	○	○
Water purification method	○	○	○	○	○
Water container	○	○	○	○	○
Coffeepot	○	○	○	○	○
Coffee filter	○	○	○	○	○
Dish towels	○	○	○	○	○
Scouring pad	○	○	○	○	○
Self-sealing plastic bags	○	○	○	○	○
Rope for tying food pack up in tree	○	○	○	○	○
Other	○	○	○	○	○

18 TRIP PLANNER

	Date	Date	Date	Date	Date
STAPLES					
Powdered milk or creamer	○	○	○	○	○
Ground coffee	○	○	○	○	○
Teabags	○	○	○	○	○
Herbal teabags	○	○	○	○	○
Hot chocolate mix	○	○	○	○	○
Fruit drink mix	○	○	○	○	○
Butter or margarine	○	○	○	○	○
Cooking oil	○	○	○	○	○
Lemons or lemon juice	○	○	○	○	○
Honey	○	○	○	○	○
Maple syrup	○	○	○	○	○
Other	○	○	○	○	○

The Camp, Grand Falls (detail), Frederick Jones, 1860

	Date	Date	Date	Date	Date
SPICE KIT					
Salt and pepper	○	○	○	○	○
Cayenne	○	○	○	○	○
Paprika	○	○	○	○	○
Mustard	○	○	○	○	○
Garlic bud	○	○	○	○	○
Parsley flakes	○	○	○	○	○
Basil	○	○	○	○	○
Herbes de Provence	○	○	○	○	○
Other	○	○	○	○	○
Plastic bags	○	○	○	○	○
Pack	○	○	○	○	○

Camping gear checklist

Nine nights passed in the open air, or on rocks and on boards, had spoiled me for the comforts of civilisation, and to sleep on a bed was impossible; I was smothered, I was suffocated, and altogether wretched and fevered; — I sighed for my rock on Lake Huron.

Anna Brownell Jameson, an Englishwoman who in 1836 traveled by canoe for nine days along the shores of Lake Huron, from *Winter Studies and Summer Rambles in Canada*

In a glade our camp is made, inside our tents we arrange the mosquito-bar (a tent within a tent looking something like a good-sized dog-kennel), and here we lie in our blankets. The hum of the foiled mosquito is unction to our souls. It is a relief, too, to remove the day's clothing, the first time in ninety-six hours.

Agnes Deans Cameron, *The New North: An Account of a Woman's 1908 Journey Through Canada to the Arctic*

	Date	Date	Date	Date	Date
	....	....	....	....	....
Tent	○	○	○	○	○
Tent poles and pegs	○	○	○	○	○
Ground cloth	○	○	○	○	○
Tarp and rope	○	○	○	○	○
Spare flashlight batteries	○	○	○	○	○
Small trowel for digging latrine	○	○	○	○	○
Pack	○	○	○	○	○

It is from this point on that we raise the sails for an afternoon of great relaxation. The wind carried us over 15-20 km. Bob Vernier, our in-house sail expert, has engineered us an efficient sailboard from dead birch branches as mast and boom, a large tarp as a sail, one paddle as an adjustable keel, one as a rudder, and ropes to maneuver the sail.
It took almost an hour to build, but was well worth the effort.

Jaclin Dufresne, June 27, 1992 journal entry,
Missinaibi River trip, northern Ontario

The Interior of the Canadian Division at the Great Exhibition of 1851, Alfred Perry, 1851

First-aid kit checklist

There are many different kinds of prepackaged first-aid kits available. However, if you are making up your own, be sure to keep it in a waterproof container and replace any items that have been used. Keep an eye on expiry dates as well.

Third Rapid on the Moisie River (detail), William Hind, 1861

	Date	Date	Date	Date	Date
Antibiotic ointment	○	○	○	○	○
Antihistamine	○	○	○	○	○
Antiseptic	○	○	○	○	○
Blister pad or moleskin	○	○	○	○	○
Calamine lotion or cream	○	○	○	○	○
Decongestant tablets	○	○	○	○	○
First-aid manual	○	○	○	○	○
General medical supplies	○	○	○	○	○
butterfly dressings	○	○	○	○	○

The medicine chest, equipped according to the formula of the Company's doctor in London, contained: two pounds of epsom salts (crystals), one dozen purgative powders, one dozen vomits (in little packets), one small spirits smelling salts, one half dozen bottles pain-killer (medium size), one or two rolls of sticking plaster, lancet, a pair of forceps. With these drugs was a book of instructions. But none of the men, not even the guide, could read them. However, they knew the doses of everything by heart. A guide never gave a man medicine to administer to himself. He was required to fetch his pannikin — a tin dish that held a pint — filled with river water, and the guide poured out what he estimated as a dose. This the patient had to drink under his observation. This was to prevent men from shamming sickness. There was very little deception practised however. When it came to extracting a tooth, the guide set his patient up against the side of the boat, got a firm grip on the tooth and hauled it out. A jack-knife was all that was required for an amputation. Everything was managed very well.

William Cornwallis King,
Hudson's Bay Company clerk, 1863

	Date	Date	Date	Date	Date
cotton wool	○	○	○	○	○
elastic (tensor) bandage	○	○	○	○	○
gauze bandage and pads	○	○	○	○	○
large sterile dressings	○	○	○	○	○
safety pins	○	○	○	○	○
scissors	○	○	○	○	○
small adhesive dressings	○	○	○	○	○
sterile eye pad	○	○	○	○	○
tape	○	○	○	○	○
triangular bandage	○	○	○	○	○
tweezers	○	○	○	○	○
Hydrocortisone cream	○	○	○	○	○
Pain-relief medication	○	○	○	○	○
Seasickness remedy	○	○	○	○	○
Space blanket	○	○	○	○	○
Stomach-upset remedy	○	○	○	○	○
Other	○	○	○	○	○

Photography gear checklist

Minutes later we were a quarter mile offshore in swells of at least eight feet. At that point we decided that fun was fun but that we weren't in control any longer....

Given this predicament, Steve took the next logical step. Pulling his camera out from under the protective cover, he turned around and snapped a picture of me. In the seconds that it took to complete this, without Steve's paddle controlling the front, the canoe swung precariously to the left and a wave washed over our breached canoe. Steve dropped the camera onto his lap and we brought the boat back into position. I breathed again. The picture is nice, but a bit out of focus.

American canoeist Scott Anderson, on the northeastern shore of Lake Winnipeg in 1987 on a trip from Duluth to York Factory, from his book *Distant Fires*, 1990

Aside from the fact that like Scott Anderson, we've all probably experienced times when taking a simple picture from a canoe or kayak has turned into a heart-stopping moment, the biggest problem with taking a camera on a trip is keeping it accessible and dry. There are three ways of doing this. A Pelikan case is waterproof, strong and floats, but it is also bulky and not exactly immediately accessible when you see that moose. Inflatable bags are another option. They are waterproof, light and can float, but they are not puncture proof and can be quite bulky. The third method is a quick-seal plastic bag. Although it is probably the most accessible way to protect your camera, it doesn't offer any other protection and doesn't float.

Film should always be kept in its plastic container before and after it is used. All film should be stored in a waterproof bag, and both camera and film should be kept out of the sun and away from heat.

Henry David Thoreau once wrote that "a man has not seen a thing until he has felt it," and he was said to have been scornful of those who saw nothing in nature but a picture. These are fair comments. We go to Lake Superior because we do indeed want to "feel" the land we are photographing. Our compulsion to use cameras and to record pleasurable experiences and phenomena is secondary to the simple joy of being there.

John and Janet Foster, *Adventures in Wild Canada,* 1984

	Date	*Date*	*Date*	*Date*	*Date*
	....	....	....	....	....
Camera and case	○	○	○	○	○
Tripod	○	○	○	○	○
Lenses	○	○	○	○	○
Lens-cleaning brush	○	○	○	○	○
Film	○	○	○	○	○
Storage bag or container	○	○	○	○	○
Spare batteries	○	○	○	○	○
Spare camera	○	○	○	○	○

Tackle checklist

That night we camped at the island in Canoe Lake ... and the next morning we went on down through Tea Lake into the Oxtongue River. Since it was towards the end of July, I knew the water was too warm for trout in most places, but that we stood a good chance of getting some where the main course was joined by a small stream.... In spite of my knowledge of the district, Mr. Adams was sure that he knew better than I did about the best places. "I've fished in almost every country except Canada," he kept saying, "and I always like a little riffle on the surface of the water...." Finally he decided to give up for that day. He had had very bad luck but it was his own fault.
Next morning, when we started out again, I decided that the best place for us to try was Salmon's Pool ... we stayed all day long. When he had thirteen, he decided it was time to go back to camp. As we returned he remarked with a happy sigh, "My cup is full."

Mark Robinson, an Algonquin Park ranger in the early 1900s

If you are a real angler, you will want to take your favorite rod with you on any canoe trip and will be happy to tie it in the canoe. If you are only a casual angler, you may wish to take a telescopic rod stowed safely inside your pack.

	Date	Date	Date	Date	Date
	....	....	....	....	....
Rod	○	○	○	○	○
Line	○	○	○	○	○
Hooks	○	○	○	○	○
Weights	○	○	○	○	○
Lures	○	○	○	○	○
Live bait	○	○	○	○	○
Filet knife	○	○	○	○	○
Fishing license	○	○	○	○	○

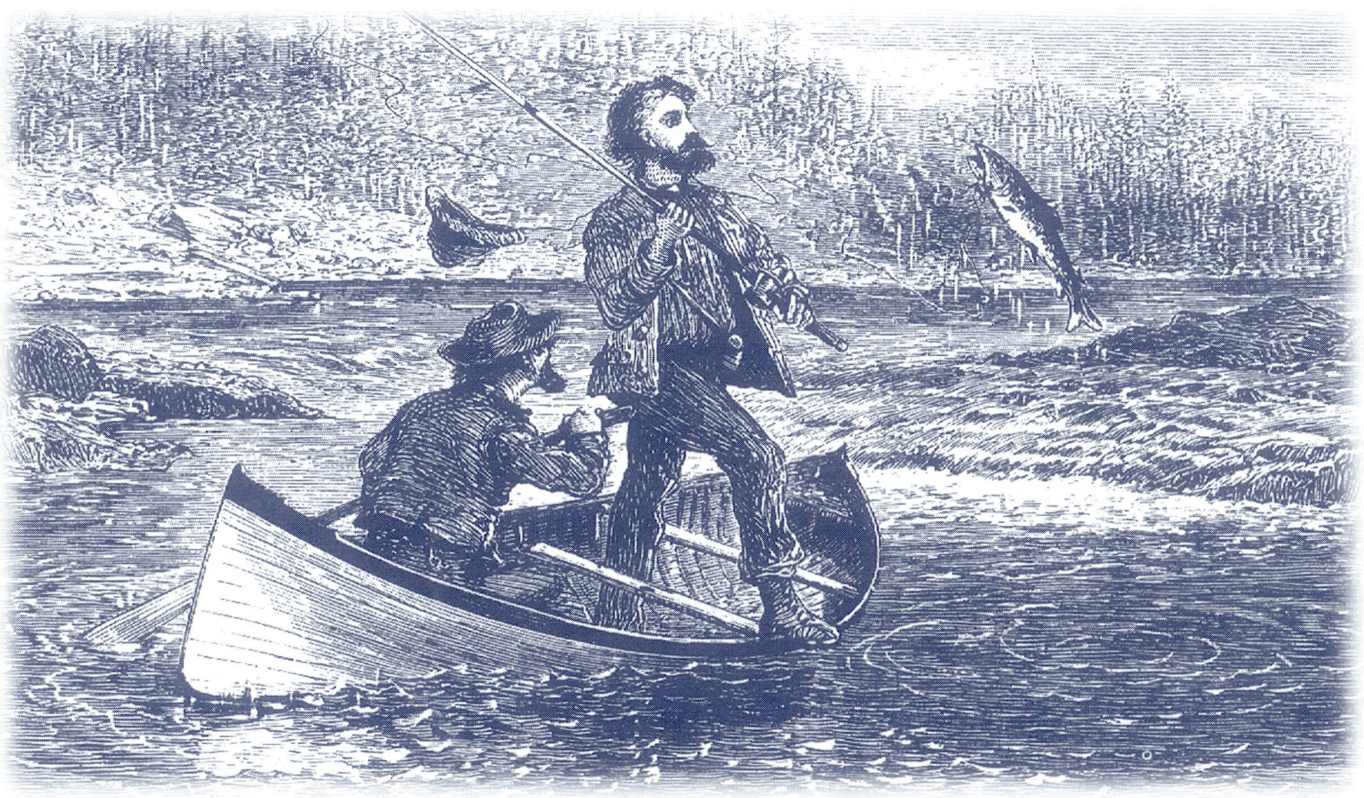

Equipment

Tumbled out at 6 sharp and were off at 6:30. We were soon in Back Lake across which we paddled about 2 1/2 miles and went into the river again. Soon the rapids commenced. We ran some all loaded (shipped water at some). At the other three we four got out and the Indians ran the canoes down with full loads. On the last rapid they must have struck a rock for by the time we reached Trout Falls at 11 a.m. both canoes were leaking considerably. Repairs had to be made. Several patches were made of tin from tin cans, the Indians carrying tacks and white lead only with them.

Kenneth C. Campbell, August 11, 1911, entry in his journal from a trip made with three friends and four guides to York Factory on Hudson Bay, *The Beaver*, August-September 1992

EQUIPMENT	Date	Date	Date	Date	Date
Canoe	O	O	O	O	O
Paddles	O	O	O	O	O
Spare paddle	O	O	O	O	O
Sail	O	O	O	O	O
PFDs (personal flotation devices)	O	O	O	O	O
Bungie cords	O	O	O	O	O
Rope	O	O	O	O	O
Bailer	O	O	O	O	O
Sponge	O	O	O	O	O
Map	O	O	O	O	O
Waterproof map case	O	O	O	O	O
Compass	O	O	O	O	O
Mirror for signaling	O	O	O	O	O
Whistle	O	O	O	O	O

Morning Scene on Lake, William Hind, 1861

	Date	Date	Date	Date	Date
Flares	○	○	○	○	○
Knee pads	○	○	○	○	○
Other	○	○	○	○	○

Repair Kit

Duct tape	○	○	○	○	○
Fiberglass repair kit	○	○	○	○	○
Epoxy	○	○	○	○	○
Sewing kit with stitching awl	○	○	○	○	○
Dental floss	○	○	○	○	○
Copper wire	○	○	○	○	○
Vise grips	○	○	○	○	○
Swiss Army knife	○	○	○	○	○
Other	○	○	○	○	○

Miscellaneous

Reservation information	○	○	○	○	○

Personal gear

I had been assigned a personal servant, Noel, who was repacking his dunnage bag. I noticed that he had one three-point Hudson's Bay blanket, a pair of ten-ounce duck trousers and duck frock — this was a kind of shirt that hung loose over the trousers — a small towel, a cake of soap, a comb, a looking-glass and a couple of pairs of moccasins. These fellows certainly could travel light. Yet, what more did a man need?

William Cornwallis King, Hudson's Bay Company clerk, recalling his 2,000-mile trip with the Red River boat brigade from Lower Fort Garry to Fort Simpson, 1863, *The Beaver*, August-September 1995

	Date	Date	Date	Date	Date
	....	....	....	....	....
CLOTHING					
Long pants	○	○	○	○	○
Shorts	○	○	○	○	○
T-shirt(s)	○	○	○	○	○
Long-sleeved shirt(s)	○	○	○	○	○
Sweater(s)	○	○	○	○	○
Sweatshirt	○	○	○	○	○
Rain jacket	○	○	○	○	○
Rain pants	○	○	○	○	○
Wool socks	○	○	○	○	○
Shoes (two pairs)	○	○	○	○	○
Underwear	○	○	○	○	○
Hats (sun hat and woolen hat)	○	○	○	○	○

Once we agreed on the menu and the equipment, two weeks were enough to gather and prepare everything. Except for personal clothes, everything was packed in respective packs one week prior to departure. This exercise allowed us to see if we could fit everything in the two canoe bags and the two barrels we intended on bringing along....

Many friends tell me they prefer spontaneity to structured preparation while planning their vacations. I tend to subscribe to the philosophy that planning is just as much part of the trip as the trip itself. Not only does planning ensure that details are not overlooked, but it also brings us closer to realizing our goal.

Jaclin Dufresne, 1992 journal entry,
Missinaibi River trip, northern Ontario

	Date	*Date*	*Date*	*Date*	*Date*
OPTIONAL CLOTHING					
Bathing suit	○	○	○	○	○
Gloves	○	○	○	○	○
Sleepwear	○	○	○	○	○
Change of clothing, left in car, for after trip	○	○	○	○	○
Bug hat	○	○	○	○	○
PERSONAL TOILET KIT					
Towel	○	○	○	○	○
Toilet roll	○	○	○	○	○
Toothbrush and paste	○	○	○	○	○
Soap and shampoo	○	○	○	○	○
Brush or comb	○	○	○	○	○
Sunscreen and lip salve	○	○	○	○	○
Bug repellent	○	○	○	○	○
Prescribed medication	○	○	○	○	○
Sewing kit	○	○	○	○	○

32 Canoeing Checklists

See also pages 14 to 26 for Food; Camp Kitchen; Camping Gear; First-Aid Kit; Photography Gear; and Tackle Checklists.

	Date	Date	Date	Date	Date
Sleep Gear					
Sleeping bag	○	○	○	○	○
Sleeping mat	○	○	○	○	○
Pillow	○	○	○	○	○
Miscellaneous					
Sunglasses	○	○	○	○	○
Camera	○	○	○	○	○
Film	○	○	○	○	○
Binoculars	○	○	○	○	○
Flashlight	○	○	○	○	○
Pocket knife	○	○	○	○	○
Spare prescription glasses	○	○	○	○	○
Personal water bottle	○	○	○	○	○
Books, cards, etc.	○	○	○	○	○
Journal and pen	○	○	○	○	○
Other	○	○	○	○	○

Portage on the Moisie, William Hind, 1861

Equipment

This equipment list covers all possibilities; obviously, for short river and lake trips, some of this equipment is not necessary.

[Gino] Watkins may be the only man who has succeeded in preserving an Edwardian elegance while in a kayak. His main contribution to Arctic exploration was that he, like Stefansson and Hearne, adopted the ways of the Inuit. This enabled him to travel light and to live off the land and sea in a way that Franklin's ill-fated expeditions could not. He was one of the first Europeans to learn to do the Eskimo roll in a kayak [in early 1930s].

C. E. S. Franks, *The Canoe and White Water*, 1977

EQUIPMENT	Date	Date	Date	Date	Date
Kayak	○	○	○	○	○
Paddle	○	○	○	○	○
Spare paddle	○	○	○	○	○
Paddle leash	○	○	○	○	○
Drip rings	○	○	○	○	○
Sprayskirt	○	○	○	○	○
Buoyancy bags	○	○	○	○	○
PFD (personal flotation device)	○	○	○	○	○
Sponge	○	○	○	○	○
Bilge pump	○	○	○	○	○
Pogies	○	○	○	○	○
Sea sock	○	○	○	○	○
Stirrup sling or paddle float	○	○	○	○	○
Dry storage bags	○	○	○	○	○

The boats of these Aleuts are about two fathoms long, two feet high and two feet wide from above; in the front, at the prow, they are pointed, at the stern the sides form an angle. Evidently the frame consists of two longitudinal poles which are joined at the ends and kept apart by cross bars. The frame is covered outside, as it seems, with seal-skins and painted a dark brown colour.... About two arshins [four feet, eight inches] from the stern there is a round opening with a skirt of whale's guts. By means of a cord, put through a hem, the lower border of the skirt may be tightly bound around the edge of the hatch while down in the hatch and stretching out his legs the American draws the upper hem of the skirt around his body under the armpits and ties it with a noose; thus the water cannot penetrate into the boat.

Georg Steller, scientist on Vitus Bering's expedition, 1741

	Date	Date	Date	Date	Date
Bungee cords / rope	◯	◯	◯	◯	◯
Charts / tide and current tables	◯	◯	◯	◯	◯
Compass	◯	◯	◯	◯	◯
Signaling mirror	◯	◯	◯	◯	◯
Flares / air horn / whistle	◯	◯	◯	◯	◯
VHF radio transceiver	◯	◯	◯	◯	◯

Repair Kit

Kayak repair kit	◯	◯	◯	◯	◯
Duct tape / wire	◯	◯	◯	◯	◯
Epoxy / sealant	◯	◯	◯	◯	◯
Vise grips	◯	◯	◯	◯	◯
Screwdriver	◯	◯	◯	◯	◯
Hacksaw blade	◯	◯	◯	◯	◯
Strapping tape	◯	◯	◯	◯	◯
Extra rudder cable and parts	◯	◯	◯	◯	◯
Extra nuts, bolts, screws	◯	◯	◯	◯	◯

Personal gear

Our neoprene reef boots were probably our most prized pieces of clothing. I couldn't imagine paddling in anything else. To enter our kayaks each day we had to step into the ice-cold water. The shock of it takes one's breath away, but within minutes our body heat warmed the neoprene and our feet stayed toasty warm all day. Wet, but warm.

Victoria Jason, *Kabloona in the Yellow Kayak: One Woman's Journey Through the Northwest Passage*, 1995

	Date	Date	Date	Date	Date
CLOTHING					
Pants	○	○	○	○	○
T-shirt(s)	○	○	○	○	○
Long-sleeved shirt	○	○	○	○	○
Short-sleeved shirt	○	○	○	○	○
Sweater	○	○	○	○	○
Sweatshirt	○	○	○	○	○
Vest	○	○	○	○	○
Jacket	○	○	○	○	○
Underwear	○	○	○	○	○
Long underwear	○	○	○	○	○
Socks	○	○	○	○	○
Hat	○	○	○	○	○
Gloves	○	○	○	○	○

	Date	Date	Date	Date	Date
Wet suit	○	○	○	○	○
Dry suit	○	○	○	○	○
Rain suit	○	○	○	○	○
Footwear	○	○	○	○	○
Bathing suit	○	○	○	○	○
Sleepwear	○	○	○	○	○
Other	○	○	○	○	○

Personal Toilet Kit

Towel	○	○	○	○	○
Toilet roll	○	○	○	○	○
Toothbrush and paste	○	○	○	○	○
Soap and shampoo	○	○	○	○	○
Brush or comb	○	○	○	○	○
Nail clippers	○	○	○	○	○
Sunscreen	○	○	○	○	○
Lip salve	○	○	○	○	○

38 KAYAKING CHECKLISTS

	Date	Date	Date	Date	Date
	....	....	....	....	....

See also pages 14 to 26 for Food; Camp Kitchen; Camping Gear; First-Aid Kit; Photography Gear; and Tackle Checklists.

	Date	Date	Date	Date	Date
Bug repellent	○	○	○	○	○
Personal medication	○	○	○	○	○
Other	○	○	○	○	○

SLEEP GEAR

Sleeping bag	○	○	○	○	○
Sleeping mat	○	○	○	○	○
Pillow	○	○	○	○	○

MISCELLANEOUS

Sunglasses	○	○	○	○	○
Waterproof watch	○	○	○	○	○
Spare prescription glasses	○	○	○	○	○
Personal water bottle	○	○	○	○	○
Other	○	○	○	○	○

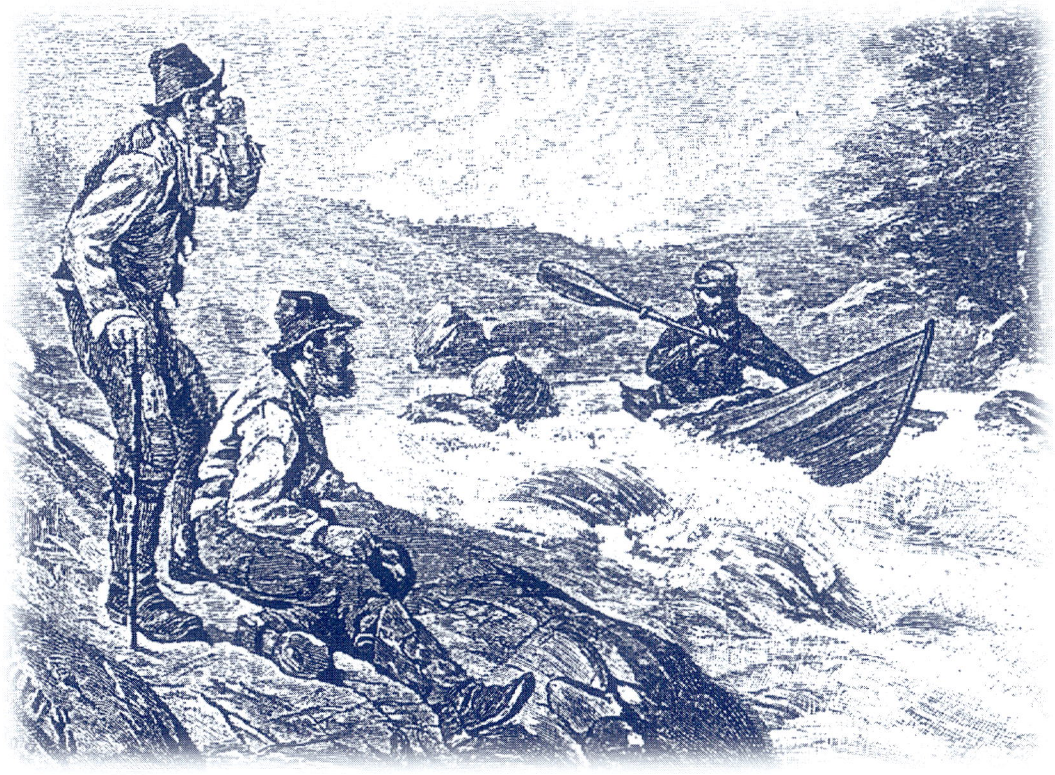

Camp stoves and wood fires

This song of the waters is audible to every ear, but there is other music in these hills, by no means audible to all. To hear even a few notes of it you must first live here for a long time, and you must know the speech of hills and rivers. Then on a still night, when the campfire is low and the Pleiades have climbed over the rimrocks, sit quietly and listen for a wolf to howl, and think hard of everything you have seen and tried to understand. Then you may hear it — a vast pulsing harmony — its score inscribed on a thousand hills, its notes the lives and deaths of plants and animals, its rhythms spanning the seconds and the centuries.

Aldo Leopold, *A Sand County Almanac*, 1949

At the end of a hard day's paddling, what most of us want is a roaring wood fire that we can stand around, fiddle with, put more wood on, dry our wet sneakers by and cook our evening meal on. Some paddlers make an art out of collecting just the right kindling — birchbark picked up along the way (never from live trees), tiny dead branches on the trunks of evergreens, pine needles. While these purists pride themselves on starting their fires with one match, other campers use a candle as a fire starter and hope for the best.

Unfortunately, for environmental reasons, on many canoe routes wood fires are no longer possible and stoves are used in their place. Even where campfires are allowed, the lightweight stove comes in handy on cold, wet days when hot food or a hot drink is needed fast.

The backwoods cook must answer one simple question before choosing a stove: does it simmer or roar? If you only use dehydrated food on your trips, all you need is a roarer, but if you cook real food, a simmerer is what you need. Stoves using white gas, (naptha gas, Coleman fuel) are roarers. Although most require priming, which can be a bit of a nuisance, they are unaffected by

In a soaking rain, starting a fire is often a group effort. Three or four days of steady drizzle will wet even the sheltered thicket tinder. You can try looking under large dead logs and other out-of-the-way places, but it may be easiest to rely on shavings from the splits of logs big enough to have a dry inner core. Preparation becomes a matter of meticulous care: at this particular campsite, Rug was quartering the splits, then splitting the quarters and slicing tinderlike splits off of those. Jim had taken a couple of the bigger splits under the fire tarp and was whittling shaving after shaving with his hunting knife.

James West Davidson and John Rugge, *The Complete Wilderness Paddler*, 1983

elevation or temperature. Butane or propane stoves require no priming and simmer well; however, they don't work well in cold temperatures.

After you've purchased a stove, practice putting it together and lighting it in various weather conditions at home before taking it out in the wild. All stoves occasionally require some maintenance and most come with a maintenance kit.

As for cooking on a camp stove, food can scorch easily in lightweight cookware, so stir a little more than usual. If you have a one-burner stove, prepare rice, pasta and other foods that cook in boiling water first and remove from heat to continue cooking while preparing the main course. Commercial devices for baking outdoors are available, although some people simply cover the pan holding the cake or bread with another pan or aluminum foil plate to hold the heat in.

Songs, tales and customs

This day we had a most delightful run among hundreds of islands; sometimes darting through narrow rocky channels, so narrow that I could not see the water on either side of the canoe; and then emerging, we glided through vast fields of white water-lilies; it was perpetual variety, perpetual beauty, perpetual delight and enchantment, from hour to hour. The men sang their gay French songs, the other canoe joining in the chorus.

Anna Brownell Jameson, *Winter Studies and Summer Rambles in Canada,* 1838

SONGS

En roulant ma boule

(A-rolling my ball)

En rou-lant ma bou-le rou-lant, En roulant ma bou - le,

Der-rièr'chez nous, ya - t - un é - tang, En roulant ma bou-le,

Trois beaux canards s'en vont baignant,rou-li,roulant,ma boule roulant.

En roulant ma boule roulant,
　En roulant ma boule.
En roulant ma boule roulant,
　En roulant ma boule.

Derrièr' chez nous, ya-t-un étang,
　En roulant ma boule.

Derrièr' chez nous, y'-t-un étang,
　En roulant ma boule.
Trois beaux canards s'en vont baignant,
Rouli, roulant, ma boule roulant,
En roulant ma boule roulant,
　En roulant ma boule.

Trois beaux canards s'en vont
　baignant,　　　　　　　}repeat
　En roulant ma boule.
Le fils du roi s'en va chassant,
Rouli, *etc.*

Le fils du roi s'en va chassant,　}repeat
　En roulant ma boule.
Avec son grand fusil d'argent,
Rouli, *etc.*

Avec son grand fusil d'argent, } *repeat*
    En roulant ma boule.
Visa le noir, tua le blanc,
Rouli, *etc.*

Visa le noir, tua le blanc, } *repeat*
    En roulant ma boule.
O fils du roi, tu es méchant!
Rouli, *etc.*

O fils du roi, tu es méchant! } *repeat*
    En roulant ma boule.
D'avoir tué mon canard blanc,
Rouli, *etc.*

D'avoir tué mon canard blanc, } *repeat*
    En roulant ma boule.
Par dessous l'aile il perd son sang,
Rouli, *etc.*

Par dessous l'aile il perd son sang, } *repeat*
    En roulant ma boule.
Par les yeux lui sort'nt des diamants,
Rouli, *etc.*

Par les yeux lui sort'nt des diamants, } *repeat*
    En roulant ma boule.
Et par le bec l'or et l'argent,
Rouli, *etc.*

Et par le bec l'or et l'argent, } *repeat*
    En roulant ma boule.
Toutes ses plum's s'en vont au vent,
Rouli, *etc.*

Toutes ses plum's s'en vont au vent, } *repeat*
    En roulant ma boule.
Trois dam's s'en vont les ramassant,
Rouli, *etc.*

Trois dam's s'en vont les ramassant, } *repeat*
    En roulant ma boule.
C'est pour en faire un lit de camp,
Rouli, *etc.*

C'est pour en faire un lit de camp, } *repeat*
    En roulant ma boule.
Pour y coucher tous les passants.
Rouli, roulant, ma boule roulant,
    En roulant ma boule roulant,
    En roulant ma boule.

Baptism

In mid-river we join the ancient force
of mud and leaves moving in their journey
down the face of the continent and after
the first dance of leaving
one element for another, we fall quiet,
waiting for the silence to give us a
glimpse of history. In mid-river, it is
still possible to imagine Thompson's world,
without roads or bridges, rivers that
go back beyond white lives into the rocks
that push and fold, fault and break
as the new world rises from
the old.
    Yet this is still our river.
It does not matter that we are not
the first, what we will find today
has been found a hundred times before: it is
the ancient story of men meeting water,

as if there were a time, or faith,
when all of us were rivers, one
strength sliding out of the sky and into
the sea, one direction in us all.

But the river churns here and beats along the shore.
It picks up speed on the outside curve
cutting past the cottonwoods and under the deadfalls
that sweep across the water like the last arm of the land
and the water takes command.
I bend my paddle in my hand and my friend
digs in but there are branches like dead fingers in our faces
and there can be
no avoidance now, water comes up up and the
snag bends us down until my lungs
are in the water they are stones and I am
grabbing for the tree as if it were
my friend while the current sucks on me and my arms
go heavy as lead, a scream
goes dead in my throat, we do not

belong here, it bubbles and swallows
silt, the taste of ice,
there are blue stars somewhere and all the sounds of water
are alive and they pour in my ears,
into my eyes as if the river is already sure
how deep it will carry me,
what it will do with my skin, how it will dissolve
and burst and thin out the blood and I roll over
in a dream of clouds, willows, catch the edge
of a bank beaver's hole, brown mud like gold on my palm,
my feet still pulling for the ocean and then they find
gravel, the river rock, the river
pushes me away and I am shaking in the air again,
shaking for my friend riding the canoe's bottom
like a drunken pea pod, he grinds on the bank
a hundred yards downstream, his boots sucked off,
his body like a hole in the sand.

I breathe in the sun, take it yellow
into the body that spits grey in the river.

The baptism is over.
We have walked away without the grace of
fish or grebes, and the river is still the same.
I sit and watch the water with the oldest eyes of men:
if I trust the river, I will be
caught in it, rolled backwards into the
simplest race of all, the first, and the river is hard, it is
carnal and twists like an animal going blind in the rain,
but it leaves me pouring water from my shoe and then I see
him stand, wave, we have
first words.
Soon our paddles will bite the water but they will not
break it: our place on earth is rich enough,
the sudden rush of birdsong, our own
mid-river laughter as the warmth begins again.

Dale Zieroth, 1981

Portage on Hoarfrost River (detail),
Edward Finden, 1836

Canadian Boat-Song

Faintly as tolls the evening chime
Our voices keep tune and our oars
  keep time.
Soon as the woods on shore look dim,
We'll sing at St. Anne's our parting hymn,
Row, brothers, row, the stream runs fast,
The Rapids are near and the daylight's past.

Why should we yet our sail unfurl?
There is not a breath the blue wave to curl,
But when the wind blows off the shore,
Oh! sweetly we'll rest our weary oar.
Blow, breezes, blow, the stream runs fast,
The Rapids are near and the daylight's past.

Ottawa's tide! this trembling moon
Shall see us float over thy surges soon.
Saint of this green isle! hear our prayers,
Oh, grant us cool heavens and favouring
  airs.
Blow, breezes, blow, the stream runs fast.
The Rapids are near and the daylight's
past.

Thomas Moore, 1804, inspired by the songs of the voyageurs
on the Ottawa River

Tales for Whiners

So you think you're carrying too much ...
The voyageurs covered 500 to 600 yards between resting places on the long portages. Here is what Malcolm McLeod, the editor of Archibald McDonald's 1828 journal had to say about the loads they carried: "The ordinary load is 180 lbs. in two 'pieces,' one tied like a 'pacton,' with the small long ends of the '*Collier*,' and which lower piece is made to fit into the small of the back as it were, and to rest on the ilium, or 'upper big back-bone' of the hip. The second piece generally some bag shaped thing, or even a barrel or a box is thrown on, and rests as in a hollow, long and convenient on the back between the shoulder blades. The broad part of the *Collier* is put across the brow, the neck is slightly bent, at the angle of most resistance by the neck and spinal column, the legs as well as the body are slightly bent, but just enough for spring, and off, so loaded and trimmed, starts the man at a bound, short but quick, and which even on rough ground up hill or level, he keeps up at a rate on an average of five miles an hour. The littlest men do that easily and I never saw nor heard of one who would touch less than the standard '180'. The disgrace would be killing, and the rivalry, ever lively, of who will carry most, has called forth feats in that way that would make the traditional 'porter of Constantinople,' hide his diminished head."

And the food tastes ghastly ...
Thursday, March 24th. Raised Camp about an hour before Day break and kept polling against a strong head Wind until Sun Set having scarcely made a Mile p [per] Hour, and the most uncomfortable Days Travelling I recollect being enveloped in Clouds of Sand from Morning until Night. Our people are fed on Wretched fare, Pease & Beans, with no other Seasoning than a little Grease; the Pease and Beans are bad of the kind and occasion a Bowel complaint which keeps the people constantly running ashore instead of prosecuting the Voyage. The face of the Country we passed through to Day is Sand & Rock and the only symptom of Vegetation is a Solitary Wormwood bush here and there of

which we can barely collect sufficient to cook our Meals.

And it's too damn cold ...
Sunday, April 24th. Keen Frost during the Night and the Still Water & edges of the River covered with thin Ice; we had notwithstanding to renew our fording Work which is certainly the most disagreeable I know; passed about 9 Miles of Battures and had to Ford the River 17 times before 6 A.M.; some of the people were so benumbed with Cold that on getting out of the Water they actually could not stand; entered the Woods of the big Hill [Grande Cote] and found the Snow deep and soft we however with great labour made a couple of Miles and put up for breakfast drenched with perspiration altho' the Morn was very severe.

And you seem to have missed the portage at the end of the small bay, opposite the third island, somewhere off that large bay ...
Sunday, May 15th. Got into a very thickety country intersected with deep Swamps and small Lakes to avoid which we are compelled to Wind about in all directions. A circumstance occurred to Day which gives me much uneasiness and is likely to expose us to much inconvenience; soon after Breakfast while on the March a Red Deer appeared close to the track; the Hunters asked if they might follow to which I replied in the negative as we could not afford time, they however (my servant Tom & George Bird) struck off the Road to have a shot and we proceeded on our route for about a couple of hours conceiving they were in the rear

until the usual resting time 12 O'Clock; after ... lighting a Fire to smoke the muschetoes which assailed us in clouds I missed the Hunters but was informed by our Guide that the track was perceptible in the Grass and that they would immediately be up with us; after waiting about an hour we heard 3 Signal Shots to Windward which were immediately answered by myself & Mr McMillan (the people being asleep) but as we were by the Sound about a couple of Miles to Leeward and blowing fresh they could not of course hear the reports. We were now satisfied that the Young Men had lost our track and I dispatched our Guide, La Plante and Laverdure in various directions in search of them it being unsafe to trust the other people from the Camp as they have not the talent of finding their way through the Woods; those who were sent returned after a fruitless search of 3 hours and had some difficulty in finding their way back to us the country being quite a labyrinth so that I am obliged to give them up as lost to us for this Voyage. We however remain where we are for the remainder of the Day in case they may cast up by Morn; it is quite unnecessary to stop longer as there is no chance of their falling in with us. Their Lives are not in danger as by keeping in a North West direction they must fall on the Bow River which they can cross by Raft or Swimming and get to Carlton or they can make a Raft & drift down to Cumberland; they have plenty of Ammunition and cannot Starve, but they will suffer much as they have but one pair of Indian Shoes each and no other cloathing than their Shirts & Leather Trousers.

Sir George Simpson, journal of 1824-25, his trip from York Factory on Hudson Bay to Fort George, British Columbia

It is established for a custom of the sea and yf a ship is lost by defaulte of the lodeman the maryners may yf they please, bring the lodeman to the windlass or any other place and cut off his head withoute the maryners being bound to answer before any judge.

Black Book of the Admiralty, c. 13th century

And isn't it time for a break yet? It seems like yesterday that I was set in that stormy scene. The bitter oaths of the men punctuated the bellowing wind as the heavy combers struck the boat fore and aft, roared over the bow, drenched us to the skin. "Bail, bail!" Bruce's voice never ceased. The pitch-black night wore on. No man hesitated. Not one complained. Through the thumping seas, the men remained strong and steady in their rowing places. They were galley-slaves; Bruce their master. I sometimes wonder if there are men anywhere today — men of the breed of these Red River voyageurs!

Out of the long nervous hours a grey dawn came. At the helm, Bruce was a Viking of old come to life, standing his boat in the open sea. The men broke into song. Great joyous, lusty song. They had forgotten their thirst, their fatigue. They were triumphant.

William Cornwallis King, Hudson's Bay Company clerk, 1863, *The Beaver*, August-September 1995

Voyageur Customs

The Canadian Voyageurs when they leave one stream to follow another have a custom of pulling off their Hats and making the sign of the Cross, and one in each Brigade if not in every Canoe repeats a short Prayer. The same ceremonies are also observed by them whenever they pass a place where any one has been buried or a Cross erected, consequently those who are in the habit of voyaging up this way are obliged to say their prayers perhaps oftener than when at home, for at almost every Rapid that we have passed since we left Montreal, we have seen a number of Crosses erected, and at one I counted no less than thirty! It is truly melancholy and discouraging when I seriously reflect on the great number of my fellow creatures who have been brought to untimely ends by voyaging up this way, and yet notwithstanding such dismal spectacles which are almost constantly before our eyes, we with all eagerness of youth press forward to follow the same route, and all in hopes of gaining a little Gold!

Daniel Williams Harmon, twenty-one years old, from his journal of a trip he took in one of thirty canoes from Lachine bound for the Northwest Company's depot at Grand Portage on Lake Superior, 1800

On Lake Superior, the voyageurs used blankets or oilcloths as sails when the wind was light and blowing from the right direction. To ensure favorable winds, they made an offering to La Vieille, "the old woman of the wind" — drops of water shaken from their paddles or a bit of tobacco scattered on the water. As the offering was made, they chanted *"Souffle, souffle, la vieille"* ("Blow, blow, old woman").

It was also customary when the voyageurs reached the height of land between the St. Lawrence and Hudson Bay watersheds west of Superior to make every novice a Nor'wester. This ceremony involved dipping a cedar branch in water and waving it over the initiate. The new Nor'wester then promised never to kiss another voyageur's wife without her consent and to carry out the initiation ceremony with other newcomers when he passed that way again. Gunshots were then fired and wine served.

Women travelers with the voyageurs often found a bunch of wildflowers at their breakfast table.

No less than ten brigades, each numbering twenty canoes, used to pass through these scenes during the summer months.... I have seen four canoes sweep round a promontory suddenly and burst upon my view, while at the same moment the wild romantic song of the voyageurs, as they plied their brisk paddles struck upon my ear; and I have felt thrilling enthusiasm on witnessing 30 or 40 of these picturesque canoes ... half shrouded in the spray that flew from the bright vermilion paddles.... Alas! the forests no longer echo to such sounds ... and nought save narrow pathways over the portages, and rough wooden crosses over the graves of the travellers who perished by the way, remains to mark that such things were.

R. M. Ballantyne, *Hudson Bay*, 1879

The Governor of Red River, Hudson's Bay, Voyaging in a Light Canoe, Peter Rindisbacher, 1826

Blackflies, little blackflies ...

If you open your mouth to curse at them, they troop into it. They insinuate themselves under your clothes, down your shirt collar, up your sleeve cuffs between the buttons of your shirt bosom. And not one or a dozen but millions at a time. You can brush them off your coat sleeves in layers. In the Mississippi valley, mosquitoes are warded off by a gauze net. In our Canadian backwoods [eastern Canada], the smoke of a big fire drives them away. But up here [Manitoba], they would tear a net to shreds, and put out a fire by the mere superincumbent weight of their numbers.

Henri Julien, an artist who traveled west with the North-West Mounted Police, July 10, 1874 journal entry

Dealing with biting insects on trips is largely a matter of knowing your enemy. Blackflies are most active early in the morning and late in the afternoon. They don't bite at night, preferring hot, sunny days. Dark-colored clothing attracts them. Mosquitoes aren't fussy about the time of day they feed on humans, although they seem to be most active at dawn and dusk and on overcast, humid days. Like blackflies, they are also drawn to dark clothes, as well as to the high body temperature, perspiration and carbon dioxide produced by fidgeting campers who think flailing their arms will get rid of the pests. Deer and horseflies are attracted by movement and sweat. They tend to be most bothersome on hot, dry days.

Urban dwellers who ventured into the backwoods for a hunting or fishing trip in the late 1800s or early 1900s wore bags made of Swiss mull (a sheer fabric) over their heads to protect themselves. In 1903 on Leonidas Hubbard's expedition across the barrens of Labrador, he and his party bought cheesecloth to wear. Unfortunately, they couldn't see through it and had to wear the veils as hoods, exposing their faces to clouds of mosquitoes, blackflies and "bulldogs," large, hungry deerflies the size of a man's thumb. One friend of

The sun is high and hot. Bob's thermometer showed 32°C in the sun during our lunch break. So hot we had to jump in the water to keep from becoming insane. Worst of all, because of the abundance of flying creatures, we chose to remain fully clothed as we have done since the beginning of our journey.... This way, we can keep our supply of bug repellent for better use.... Rob Cope and I decided to dress down, but each stop to shore was a chore. You either took the time to dress up again or suffered the inconvenience of the minute beasts while it lasted. They just don't give up.

Jaclin Dufresne, June 25, 1992 journal entry, Missinaibi River trip, northern Ontario

Watercolor of surveyors crossing Mosquito Lake, Labrador, William Hind, 1861

ours who detests bug hats does roughly the same — he drapes a light towel under his hat so that it covers his neck and ears. Bug hats, bug jackets, gloves, tightly cuffed sleeves and pantlegs, zippers rather than buttons — all these protective measures are often preferable to smearing various insect-repelling potions on one's body. But when all else fails ...

Some nineteenth-century woodsmen spread a mixture of sweet oil and tar on their faces and necks. One naturalist we know recommends consuming garlic pills in the spring and summer, although garlic remedies have failed scientific bug-repelling tests. Repellents containing N,N-diethyl-m-toluamide, commonly called DEET, have been proven to repel mosquitoes and blackflies, but are less effective against deer and horseflies. Higher percentage solutions are not more repellent; they just last longer. Since this stuff is absorbed through the skin and can cause allergic and toxic reactions if used repeatedly in high concentrations, some paddlers put it on their clothing rather than on their bodies. Another alternative, oil of citronella products, provides only short-term protection. All insect repellents can be washed off by perspiration, swimming and evaporation and must be reapplied to maintain effectiveness.

The voyageurs, on the other hand, simply wore their hair long to fend off the hordes and presumably made frequent use of their favorite profanity, *saccajé chien.*

Knots

Bowline

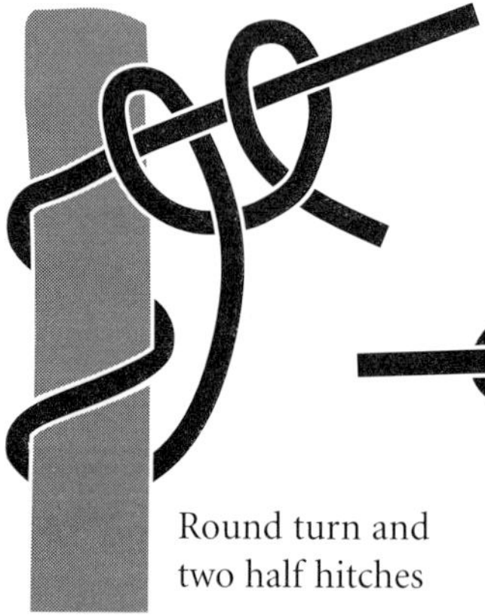

Round turn and two half hitches

Clove hitch

Reef Knot

Wherever I need to tie a knot I just make one up. Well, that's not quite true. I know a granny knot and a square knot. But when I'm in a hurry I never know which one it will be..... If you want to know about rope, that's another matter. I know a lot of things about rope. For example, ropes are always too short or too long. If the rope is too short and you tie two lengths together, you'll find that the knot is always in the wrong place and won't go through the pulley or gets caught on a branch. If the rope is too long and you cut it, you'll find that the next time you need it, both pieces will be too short.

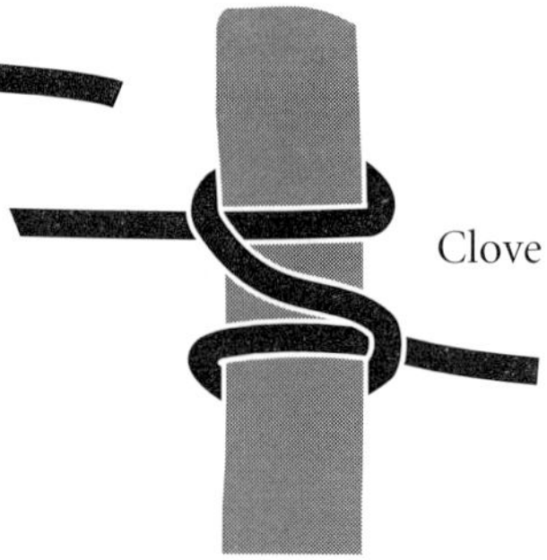

Bill Mason, *Song of the Paddle*, 1988

Running a Rapid on the Mattawa River, Frances Hopkins

Rubaboo and bannockburn

Had 'berry-pemmican' at supper. That is to say, the ordinary buffalo pemmican, with Saskatoon berries sprinkled through it at the time of making ... Take scrapings from the driest outside corner of a very stale piece of cold roast beef, add to it lumps of tallowy rancid fat, then garnish all with long human hairs (on which string pieces, like beads, upon a necklace), and short hairs of oxen, or dogs, or both, — and you have a fair imitation of common pemmican, though I should rather suppose it to be less nasty.

Pemmican is most endurable when uncooked. My men used to fry it with grease, sometimes stirring-in flour, and making a flabby mess, called "rubaboo" which I found almost uneatable. Carefully-made pemmican, such as that flavoured with the Saskatoon berries, or some that we got from the mission at St. Ann, or the sheep-pemmican given us by the Rocky Mountain hunters, is nearly good, — but, in two senses, a little of it goes a long way.

Earl of Southesk, *Saskatchewan and the Rocky Mountains: A Diary and Narrative of Travel ... in 1859 and 1860*

PEMMICAN

1 lb	dried beef	500 g
3/4 cup	Saskatoon berries, cranberries or blueberries	150 mL
	beef suet, melted	

Mince meat in a food processor or blender. Add berries and process briefly. Turn into bowl and add enough melted suet to hold beef and berries together. Cool in bowl for a few minutes, then spread out on a baking sheet and allow to cool completely. Cut into bars, wrap in plastic wrap and store in refrigerator until ready to use on trip.

BANNOCK

3/4 cup	all-purpose flour	150 mL
1/4 cup	whole-wheat flour	50 mL
1 tsp	baking powder	5 mL
1/4 tsp	salt	1 mL
	water	
	shortening or oil	

Mix together the dry ingredients (this can be done at home before the trip). Add enough cold water to make a stiff dough. Knead into a flat cake. Cook with a small amount of shortening or oil over low heat until golden brown, then turn.

From here to the Arctic are no domestic animals, the taste of beef or mutton or pork or chicken is unknown, bread gives place to bannock (with its consequent indigestion "bannockburn"), and coffee is a beverage discredited. Tobacco to smoke, strong, black, sweetened tea to drink from a copper kettle, — this is luxury's lap.

Agnes Deans Cameron, *The New North: An Account of a Woman's 1908 Journey Through Canada to the Arctic*

The tin kettle, in which they [the voyageurs] cooked their food, would hold eight or ten gallons. It was hung over the fire, nearly full of water, then nine quarts of peas — one quart per man, the daily allowance — were put in; and when they were well bursted, two or three pounds of pork, cut into strips, for seasoning, were added, and all allowed to boil or simmer till daylight, when the cook added four biscuits, broken up, to the mess, and invited all hands to breakfast. The swelling of the peas and biscuits had now filled the kettle to the brim, so thick that a stick would stand upright in it.

Capt. Thomas G. Anderson, "Personal Narrative," Wisconsin Historical Collections, 1882

Additions to Bannock: raisins, caraway seeds, a spoonful of sugar, fresh berries, dried fruit, nuts. You can also experiment with different types of flour, corn meal, bran, and wheat germ.

A Night Encampment, Robert Petley, 1837

Split Pea Soup

2 cups	split peas	500 mL
1	onion, chopped	1
1 or 2	cloves garlic, minced	1 or 2
1 tbsp	oil	15 mL
10 cups	water	2.5 L
1/2 tsp	salt	2 mL
1/4 tsp	pepper	1 mL
1	bay leaf	1
2	slices bacon, chopped and fried (optional)	2

Sort peas. Soak if package instructions say to do so. In pot, sauté onion and garlic in oil. Add peas, water, salt, pepper, bay leaf and bacon (if using). Bring to boil and simmer until puréed, stirring occasionally.

Carry in, carry out

When we arrived at one of my favorite campsites on a beautiful little island, we were confronted by the sight of 26 individual dumps, and toilet paper blowing everywhere. The island is predominantly Precambrian rock, so the cleanup took an hour and a half. It took much longer for the rage to subside.

Bill Mason, *Song of the Paddle*, 1988

No-trace camping has one goal — to protect the wilderness from the impact of human visitors. Most experienced campers will be familiar with the suggestions that follow; those who are new to wilderness tripping may want to familiarize themselves with this and other information on low-impact camping provided by outdoor stores, parks and outfitters.

Protecting the area you are paddling through begins on the first portage. The old adage "Take only pictures; leave only footprints" just doesn't work on a trail used by hundreds of people a season. Too many footprints around muddy sections can widen trails, destroying the ground cover on both sides. Keep on the trail whenever possible.

When available, choose previously-used campsites and don't alter the site to suit your own purposes (clearing vegetation, moving logs, etc.).

Camp stoves are more environmentally friendly than campfires, but if you decide to build a fire, check first that there is a safe place on which to build it (on bedrock or sand) and that there is enough deadfall in the area. Never leave a fire unattended, and always check that your campfire is truly out before leaving the site.

A reporter covering the Red River Rebellion flanked by two guides, 1870

In some parks, modified outhouses consisting of a box with a hinged lid are provided at campsites. In other wilderness areas, you're on your own. Whether you dig a hole to bury excrement, leave it on the surface or carry it out depends on the climatic and soil conditions of the area you're visiting. Find out the local etiquette before your trip.

Water in lakes and rivers can be protected by bathing and washing dishes away from the water source rather than directly in it. Try to use as little biodegradable soap as possible; sand works well as an abrasive for cleaning pots.

When you're ready to break camp, be sure you have removed all evidence of your stay — fill in and cover holes, check for garbage and carry out what you brought in.

Weather forecasting

A large loon flew by in the afternoon; its screamings which had of late been frequent are, by many, considered as sure indications of the approach of stormy weather; we heard them frequently, but had no opportunity of forming a conclusive opinion as to the degree of importance to be attached to this prognostic.

William Keating, in the Adirondacks, August 23, 1823 journal entry

Aug. 15th, 1808. At eleven o'clock [a.m.] everything was dry, and the wind had abated: we hoisted sail ... a sudden squall ... obliged us to put shore at l'Isle d'Encampement where we were detained until three o'clock ... We kept on with double-reefed sail until nine o'clock, when we camped on a fine sandy beach. We soon had a terrible squall ... My tent was blown down and we passed a wretched night, wet to the skin.

Alexander Henry (the Younger), with the Saskatchewan Brigade on Lake Winnipeg, 1801

Like sailors, shepherds and farmers, the voyageurs spent their working lives battling the elements. For their own safety and the safety of their cargoes, a knowledge of local weather patterns was mandatory. Even today, it is important to know the weather patterns of the area you plan to visit. In the planning stages of a trip, weather information (average monthly rainfall, average temperatures, relative humidity, etc.) and marine information (tides and currents) can be obtained from federal agencies. Closer to the departure date, national weather channels can be checked for long-range forecasts. On the trip itself, winds, clouds, and the sun and moon can help determine weather conditions in the upcoming days.

The two old sayings "A wind from the south brings rain in its mouth" and "When wind is in the east, 'tis good for neither man nor beast" have some scientific basis. A south or east-blowing wind generally means you're near a front. Winds that continue through the night are also a sign that unsettled weather is on the way. Winds from the west or north, on the other hand, tend to mean that you're on the eastern side of a high-pressure area and can expect

These lakes (Huron and Superior) ... are subject to sudden squalls.... Unless therefore you have time to reach the land, an upset is inevitable. Consequently it is necessary to creep around the shore; but when a bay ... is come to, the crew, naturally, to save time and labour like to strike straight across from headland to headland. As some of the traverses are not less than twenty miles broad, it is necessary to study the weather and to be an accurate judge of ... probabilities ... For the waves of Huron and Superior are not inferior in size and power to those of the ocean, if indeed, they are not more to be dreaded.

Paul Fountain, *The Great North-West and Great Lake Region of North America,* 1904

good weather in the days ahead. On large lakes, winds often rise in the afternoon, making morning and evening the best times for travel.

High, wispy cirrus clouds ("mares' tails") are frequently the first sign of rain and precede a storm by eighteen to thirty-six hours. However, towering, dense cumulonimbus clouds with surrounding lower clouds signal thunderstorms that may arrive within a few hours. "Red sky at night, sailors delight/Red sky in morning, sailors take warning" also tends to be a useful adage. In the evening, a red sky indicates a high-pressure area is likely coming from the west, while a red sky in the morning means that the good weather has already passed by and unsettled weather is sure to follow.

"A ring around the sun or moon, brings rain or snow upon you soon" is another one of the more reliable sayings. High cirrus clouds, the forerunners of wet weather, refract light through the ice crystals they contain and produce a halo around the sun or moon.

Our ancestors also noticed that animals were sensitive to weather changes and came up with the following: "Seagull, seagull, sit on the sand/It's a sign of rain when you're at hand" and "Fish leap before a storm." Even milkweed pods can help you predict the weather: they start to fold up when a storm is approaching!

Star chart

May

The sun was trembling now on the edge of the ridge. It was alive, almost fluid and pulsating, and as I watched it sink I thought that I could feel the earth turning from it, actually feel its rotation. Over all was the silence of the wilderness, that sense of oneness which comes only when there are no distracting sights or sounds, when we listen with inward ears and see with inward eyes, when we feel and are aware with our entire beings rather than our senses. I thought as I sat there of the ancient admonition "Be still and know that I am God," and knew that without stillness there can be no knowing, without divorcement from outside influences man cannot know what spirit means.

Sigurd Olson, *The Singing Wilderness*, 1956

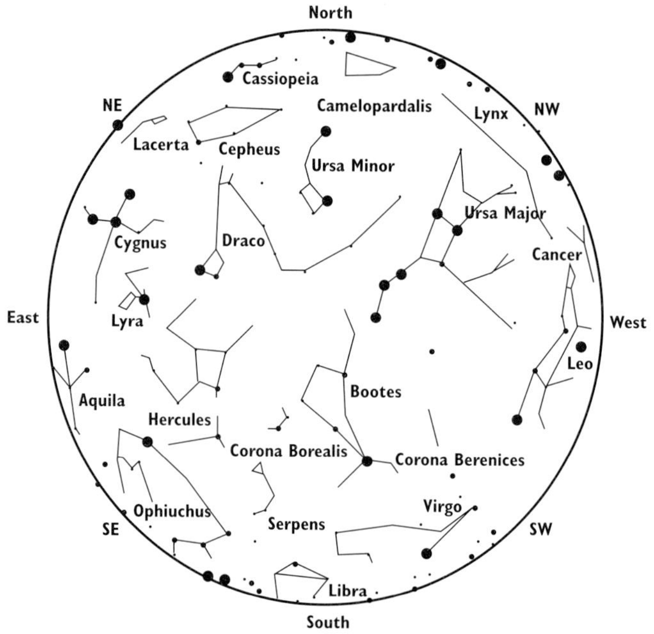

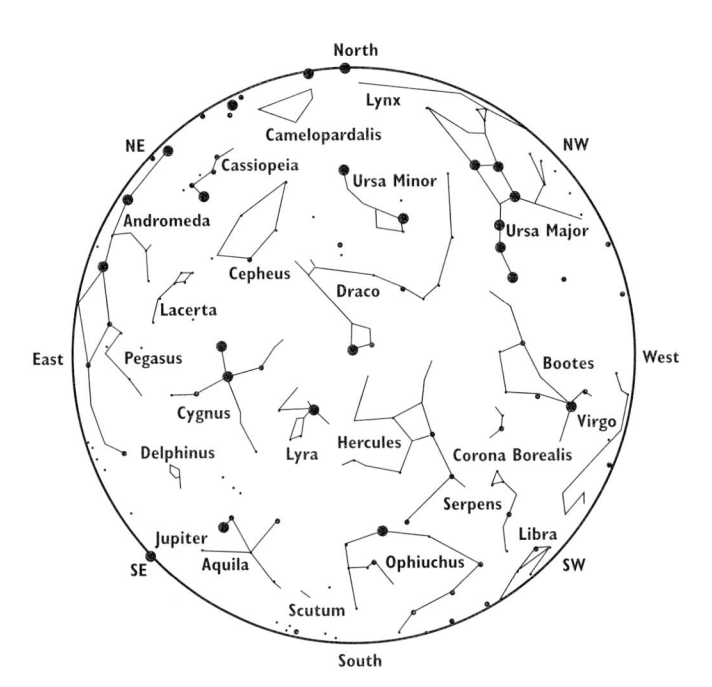

July

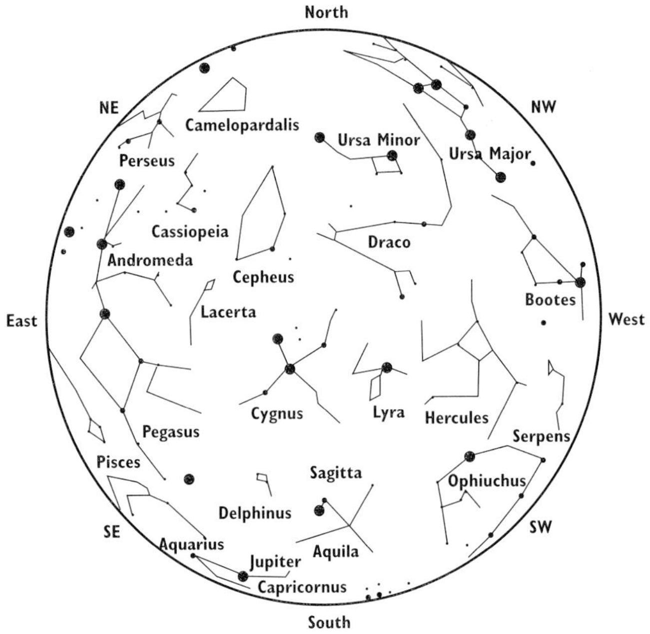

September

Bears, leeches, snakes and jellyfish

*On one of these portages, past a falls, Terk,
who was double-packing ahead, came upon a large
Barren Grounds grizzly, asleep under a willow-
bush. He wanted to say quietly to Angus, who was
following with the canoe, "Look out, there's a
grizzly," but the words wouldn't come.
At this point the bear awoke, took one startled look
at an aluminum canoe advancing on two legs, and
galloped towards the horizon like an express train.
At the top of a rise, it stopped and looked back,
snorted, and took off again.*

Eric W. Morse, *Freshwater Saga: Memoirs of a Lifetime of
Wilderness Canoeing in Canada*, 1987

Bears, leeches, poisonous snakes and stinging marine creatures are four animals that most paddlers like to encounter from afar on their trips. On the West Coast, cougars (mountain lions) are often added to the list.

Although Victoria Jason and her kayak-paddling companions were chased twice by curious polar bears along the shore of Hudson Bay in 1994, most of us portage or camp in black bear and grizzly country. It's important to remember that bears that want to eat humans are very rare. However, bears that want to eat our food are another matter entirely, particularly in years when the berry crops are poor. It's obviously unwise to camp near bear trails, which are found near berry patches and fishing streams. These trails are marked by staggered oval depressions, made as bears step in the same tracks left on previous visits. At campsites, most people suspend their food in a sturdy bag over a branch that is at least 3 yards (3 m) from the ground. The tree should be at least 110 yards (100 m) from the sleeping area. Locating tents upwind from the cooking area is another good idea, as is never taking food into a tent, keeping a clean camp and leaving the dog at home (dogs have been known to lead bears right back to camp).

May 26. So high a wind that it has prevented us from sailing much of the Day. We are encamped on an Island, of which there are many in this Lake [Lake Huron], and on one of them it is said the Natives killed a Snake that measured thirty six feet, the length and size of which they engraved on a large smooth Rock, which we saw as we passed by.

Daniel Williams Harmon, twenty-one years old, from his journal of a trip he took in one of thirty canoes from Lachine bound for the Northwest Company's depot at Grand Portage on Lake Superior, 1800

While [jellyfish] can't very well make a meal of a man, they don't know it. They just bump and sting, bump and sting. To avoid the sting, man has only to avoid the bump. While he may be able to depend on the fear, quiet good nature, or the escape "reflexes" of other potentially dangerous animals, he cannot do this with the jellyfish. He must learn to keep out of the way.

Roger Caras, *Dangerous to Man: A Definitive Story of Wildlife's Reputed Dangers*, 1975

On the trail, making noise while you walk — bear bells tied to a pack — will warn bears of your approach. If you surprise a bear in the woods, it will likely try to get away from you as quickly as it can. If it does approach or stand on its hind legs to get a better look at you, it may be curious, not aggressive. According to experts, your reaction should be to act like a human animal rather than a prey animal. Running may trigger an instinctive reaction to chase you, and since a bear can outrun an Olympic sprinter, it won't be much of a contest. Stand tall, speak in a loud low voice, back away slowly and diagonally, and avoid direct eye contact with the animal.

A bear that is protecting its young or a food source (if you smell decomposing meat in the woods, leave the area) may warn you by flattening its ears, snorting and making a short charge at you. If this happens, follow the above instructions, but act aggressively by shouting and waving your arms. Easier written about than actually done, of course.

As for cougars, government wildlife officials emphasize that these shy animals rarely attack humans and if encountered will usually run away. Nevertheless, if you're on a trail, it's a good idea to make plenty of noise to warn them of your presence. If you do encounter one, experts recommend the following: never crouch down, turn your back or run; give the animal room to escape; raise your arms to look larger; and act aggressively by throwing

I couldn't speak. My foot was black with two-inch-long wiggling leeches. They squirmed between my toes while thick clumps of tiny ones clung to the blisters like petals on a chrysanthemum. I couldn't feel a thing, but the ghastly sight was soon made worse when I swiped my boot across them. I had forgotten that leeches cling to skin with a suction-cup mouth; my foot was now streaked in blood.

Joanie McGuffin, along the Boundary Waters, 1984, from *Where Rivers Run: A 6,000-Mile Exploration of Canada by Canoe*

rocks. Again, easier to write about than to do.

Leeches, on the other hand, are completely harmless but stomach-turning little creatures. In North America, only one allergic reaction to a bite has ever been recorded. Pulling them off can lead to infection if any parts are left behind, so the recommended method of removal is to sprinkle salt on them and wait for them to curl up and drop off. In Joanie McGuffin's case, no salt was available, so her enterprising husband, Gary, sprinkled powdered soup over her foot. Other people recommend burning them at the stake with a match or cigarette. An ice cube works, too, but we just never seem to have any handy.

Northern North America's

venomous snakes — the rattlesnake, cottonmouth and copperhead — are all pit vipers. These snakes have triangle-shaped heads with a pit on each side between the eye and nostril. The coral snake, found in the southern United States, has red, yellow and black rings, the red ring touching the yellow ring. None of these snakes are aggressive animals, although they will defend themselves if threatened or injured. The best prevention against bites is precaution. Look before placing your hands under a log, into a hole or onto a branch. Watch where you place your feet while walking — step onto logs rather than over them if the ground on the other side is not visible. If you think you hear a rattlesnake, don't move until you determine where the sound is coming from. You don't want to step on the snake or move into its range. Most important, read a good snake-identification guide for the area you will be paddling through and learn to tell the poisonous varieties from the non-poisonous ones.

If someone in your group is bitten by a snake, seek medical help immediately. According to *The Outward Bound Wilderness First-Aid Handbook*, "Most medical experts agree that traditional field treatments such as tourniquets, pressure dressing, ice packs, and 'cut and suck' snakebite kits are generally ineffective and are possibly dangerous. Poisonous snakebite is one of those conditions that you cannot treat in the field. Don't waste valuable time trying."

There is a simple rule to remember when traveling along North America's coastlines: stay away from jellyfish with a lot of tentacles. They tend to be the ones that sting. As for other stinging sea creatures — coral, sea anemones, sea urchins — a good marine wildlife guide will help you identify them so that you can keep out of their way.

Animal tracks

NOT TO SCALE

Bear

Wolf

Immediately below the last rapid, we find a nice campsite where a little stream flows. There are bear and wolf tracks on the beach. Russell goes fishing again and quickly returns with a salmon and three trout, each about a foot long. We eat another great fish dinner and watch northern lights appear about 10:30. We are now at an elevation of only one hundred feet.

Paul Ferguson, "Canoeing Labrador's Notakwanon River," Coastal CaNews

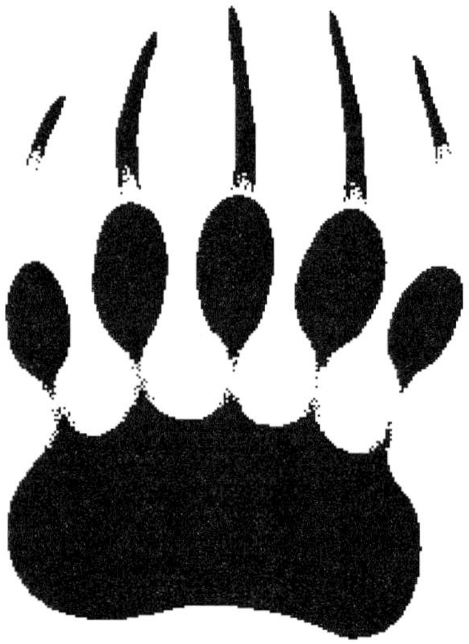

Muskrat

Otter

Porcupine

Fox

NOT TO SCALE

Deer

Mink

Beaver

69 FLORA AND FAUNA

Animal sightings

Species ....

Locale ....

Time/Date ....

Notes ....

....

....

....

....

....

> The only quadrupeds we saw were a racoon and an animal like a polecat. But the inhabitants also had the skins of bears, foxes, wolves, wild cats, deer, martens, ermine, squirrels, and of seals and sea beaver. We saw few land birds and few water fowl, and all species except ravens and crows were extremely shy and fearful, probably from being often hunted. Among the land birds is a very beautiful hummingbird.
>
> Capt. James Cook, 1778 journal entry during visit to British Columbia's Nootka Sound

Species	Locale	Time/Date	Notes

At the coast, we found Hudson Bay full of ice pans, separated by narrow channels which formed when the tide went out…. Sea creatures were much in evidence. Beluga whales swam around us, and under the canoe, which gave us a bit of a scare. They were just playing, however, and they actually seemed to be taking care not to strike the canoe, for which I was thankful. There were also numerous seals on the ice, and eider ducks nesting everywhere we looked.

Sydney Augustus Keighley, Hudson's Bay Company employee, 1934 journal entry, from
Trader, Tripper, Trapper

Bird silhouettes

NOT TO SCALE

Kingfisher

Jay

Gull

Falcon

Buteo

Accipiter

Chipewyan is a bird paradise; the whole woods are vocal to-day.....We hear the note of the ruby-crowned kinglet (regulus calendula) which some one says sounds like "Chappie, chappie, jackfish." The American red-start comes to our very feet, the yellow warbler, the Tennessee warbler, the red-eyed vireo, and the magnolia warbler, which last, a young Cree tells us, is "High-Chief-of-all-the-small-birds."...We are fortunate in getting a picture of the nest of the Gambel sparrow and two of the nesting white-throated sparrow. They are ferreted out for us by the sharp eyes of a girl who says her Cree name is "A-wandering-bolt-of-night-lightning!"

Agnes Deans Cameron, *The New North: An Account of a Woman's 1908 Journey through Canada to the Arctic*, 1986

Loon

Mallard

Merganser

Nighthawk

Owl

Swan

Whip-poor-will

Cliff swallow

73 Flora and Fauna

Not to scale

Bird sightings

Species	Locale	Time/Date	Notes

The birds above were the same species that circled the birchbark canoes of the old brigades. The voyageurs had heard the same screaming of the terns, had watched the flight of countless mallards up and down the river, had no doubt marveled as we did at the aliveness in the area.

Sigurd Olson, *The Lonely Land*, 1961, based on his canoe trip through northern Saskatchewan

Species	Locale	Time/Date	Notes

Plants to avoid along the way

The three types of contact poisonous plants in North America are common poison ivy, oakleaf poison ivy (poison oak) and poison sumac. "Leaflets three, let it be" and "Berries white, take flight" are two old sayings that should be kept in mind while walking through the woods and along river valleys. Although the rashes and blisters caused by contact with these plants are itchy and uncomfortable, they are not life-threatening — just extremely aggravating.

Each poison ivy leaf has three, often drooping, leaflets — green in the spring and summer, yellow, then red, in the fall. Its white, waxy berries also serve to

identify the plant, which grows as ground cover, a shrub or a vine. Paddlers who get into a patch shouldn't touch the exposed area — the plant's poisonous oil can be transferred from one part of the body to another. Skin that has been exposed should be washed with soap and cool water as soon as possible. Clothes that may have come into contact with the plant should also be washed. A folk remedy recommends applying the juice of jewelweed stems or leaves to the affected area to relieve the itching and heal the rash. Or simply apply rubbing alcohol and calamine lotion.

One of my guides lately made a trial of the virtue of an herb which is to be met with every where, and the knowledge of which is exceedingly necessary to travellers, not for any good qualities it possesses, for I have never as yet heard any attributed to it, but because too much care cannot be taken to avoid it ... some persons merely by looking upon it are seized with a violent fever, which lasts more than fifteen days, and is accompanied with a very troublesome scab, attended with a prodigious itching all over the body ... No remedy is as yet known for it but patience.....
Pierre-François-Xavier de Charlevoix, French explorer, *Journal of a Voyage to North-America, 1744*

We stumbled upon a brook, running merrily over a gravelly bottom, the mouth of which is imperceptible from the lake. Where it comes from and whether it may not be another mouth of the former one I cannot tell, for the ground was covered with a kind of nettle, growing very high, which, though not so painful as our English nettle, made nothing of stinging through our trousers.

John Langton, *Early Days in Upper Canada, Letters of John Langton ... 1833-37*

Poison Ivy

Poison oak grows as a low-lying shrub. Like poison ivy, each leaf has three leaflets, but they are lobed. The fruit is similar in appearance as well, although the individual berries may be covered in a soft down. Poison sumac, a treelike shrub, prefers swamps to woodland. The nonpoisonous variety has red fruit and seeds growing upward in clusters from the tips of branches, whereas the poisonous variety has white fruits and seeds that hang down in late summer and fall. Rashes from contact with both poison oak and poison sumac should be treated in the same way as those caused by poison ivy.

Stinging nettle, which grows 2 to 4 feet (0.6 to 1.2 m) high, is covered with coarse, stinging hairs. Although it is not poisonous, walking through these plants can be an uncomfortable experience, as John Langton found out many years ago.

Nettle

Poison Oak

Cooking the catch

I cleaned and prepared the fish [walleyes] and kept the fire going while absorbing the scene. When the dried potatoes and onions were simmering gently I added the fish, seasoned it with salt and pepper, added a little powdered milk and a spoonful of precious tinned butter ... Here was chowder as it is made in the North and as the Finns and Scandinavians have made it for centuries in Europe.

Sigurd Olson, *The Lonely Land*, 1961

On the same canoe trip across northern Saskatchewan, Olson also made fish cakes with leftover pike fillets and mashed potatoes from dinner. He made these before retiring for the night and left them in the pan to cook up at dawn. He and his companions ate the fish cakes next morning with porridge, so obviously no wild creature carried the tasty morsels off in the night. Olson must have covered the pan, but even so, what luck that his breakfast was still there in the morning!

Here are two other simple ways to cook freshly-caught fish: baked *en papillote* (in bag) and pan fried.

BAKED FISH
- Wash and clean fish and cut into steaks.
- Put a dab of butter and a squirt of lemon on each steak and sprinkle with herbs such as pepper, thyme, dill or fennel. Do not add too many herbs because they can overpower the delicate flavor of the fish.
- Double wrap each steak in foil and seal.
- Bake on grill or in coals of fire for 10 minutes per inch (2.5 cm) of thickness, or until fish flakes easily when pierced with a fork.
- Serve with a slice of lemon.

Camping Out, Artist Unknown, 1867

Pan-fried fish

- Wash, clean and fillet fish.
- In a plastic bag, mix flour and herbs. (This can be done at home before the trip.) Toss fillets in plastic bag until they are coated.
- Cook in butter or oil (some people use a combination of both) in frying pan until golden brown.
- Serve with a slice of lemon.

Record of fish caught

Species	Size	Number	Date	Location

There is nothing more disagreeable than a wringing wet forest in cold weather, unless it is paddling a canoe in cold rain. So that day we constructed drying racks and dried out the clothes and blankets, spending our time fishing. Before night we fixed up a stew which was to last several days. This was the combination: jackfish and beans. What a mess! But we had learned to like everything.

Eric Sevareid, age seventeen, 1930 canoe trip from Minneapolis to Hudson Bay, from *Canoeing with the Cree*, 1968

Bill tried to fish at lunchtime, but snagged his line too often in the shallows. We had to discourage trolling, too — we were going too slowly to allow time for that. In fact, we laid down some ground rules: no fishing unless the fishermen were ahead or the party was windbound. I consider it important on a canoe trip to have a schedule.

Eric W. Morse, *Freshwater Saga: Memoirs of a Lifetime of Wilderness Canoeing in Canada*, 1987

Species	Size	Number	Date	Location
....	....	....	....	....
....	....	....	....	....
....	....	....	....	....
....	....	....	....	....
....	....	....	....	....
....	....	....	....	....
....	....	....	....	....
....	....	....	....	....
....	....	....	....	....
....	....	....	....	....
....	....	....	....	....
....	....	....	....	....

Basic first aid and injury prevention

If we have a tendency to be critical of the people involved in wilderness accidents, we should maybe remind ourselves that all such accidents could be avoided by simply staying at home. For most of my acquaintances this little piece of advice would go over like a lead balloon. We know there are risks out there and we know that anyone can make a mistake. It may be an unavoidable mistake or a stupid one. It just makes sense to eliminate the risks as much as we can and to learn from the mistakes of others. The physical, mental, and spiritual enjoyment derived from a wilderness journey is worth all the risks.

Bill Mason, *Path of the Paddle*, 1980

Keeping well on a canoe or kayak trip is largely a matter of common sense. During strenuous activity, especially on hot days, it makes sense to drink 3/4 to 1 gallon (3 to 4 L) of water to prevent dehydration. Dark yellow urine, a decrease in urine, thirst, apathy, headaches and dry mucous membranes in the nose and mouth are all signs of dehydration. Obviously, it also makes sense to be sure that the water you drink is actually drinkable. It's better to be safe than sorry when it comes to giardiasis (beaver fever), a parasitic infection with symptoms that mimic influenza's. About ten minutes of boiling makes water safe to drink (shake the cooled water up to re-aerate it) or treat water with iodine tincture or tablets (add lemon or lime to improve the taste) or with a filter. Paddling and portaging use muscles that we may not use regularly. Our backs are particularly at risk. It's important to strengthen stomach muscles before a trip, but equally important to lift properly — bent knees with hips and toes aligned — when on the trip. Stretching every day should be standard practice, too. All paddlers should watch out for signs of hypothermia in their companions. There are two basic types of hypothermia. In the first type, gradual exposure, steady heat loss takes place in a cold environment through respiration, evaporation (sweat, wet clothes), or inadequate insulation. In the second type, acute immersion, rapid heat loss takes place in cold water, where the body cools up to twenty-five times faster than in air. In the early stages of mild hypothermia, vigorous shivering is usually accompanied by increased pulse and breathing rates. Cold, white hands and feet are the first signs of blood being shunted away from the body's extremities to the vital organs. Pay close attention to anybody who is confused, abnormally clumsy, paddling off-course, or otherwise behaving erratically.

Obviously, wearing appropriate clothing for cold and wet conditions is key to preventing hypothermia. A thermos of hot tea or chocolate will prevent the onset of mild hypothermia. However, if one of your group is displaying signs of mild hypothermia, replace wet clothing with dry layers, covering the head and neck; shelter the person from cold and wind; supply hot sugared liquids (no alcohol) and food (candy bars); get the person moving — physical activity generates muscle heat. If the person is getting stiff, has stopped shivering and is either unconscious or showing signs of clouded consciousness (slurred speech or severe loss of coordination), remove any wet or damp clothing; wrap the person warmly in a space blanket and sleeping bag; keep the head covered; keep the person lying flat; and seek medical help immediately.

Protection from the sun involves wearing a hat, protective clothing, plenty of sunscreen and sunglasses. To treat sunburn, apply cool compresses to the burned area; soak in cool water; take a pain reliever to reduce pain; apply calamine lotion; if blisters form, don't break them intentionally; if blisters do break, apply an antibiotic ointment and cover with a sterile dressing.

Two final points for traveling safely. First, never let the aim to make a certain destination take priority over safety. Cold, hungry, tired paddlers are a recipe for disaster, as is ignoring worsening weather conditions. And second, always keep an emergency first-aid handbook in your first-aid kit.

Signalling in an emergency

North Canoe Running Tanner's Rapid, Maligne River, William Napier, 1857

If ye find a beaten game trail, ye follow that an' it'll bring ye to water — that is, if ye go the right way, an' that ye know by its gettin' stronger. If it's peterin' out, ye'r goin' in the wrong direction. A flock of Ducks or a Loon going over is sure to be pointing for water. Y're safe to follow.... But come right down to it, the compass is the safest thing. The sun and stars is next, an' if ye know your friends will come ye'r best plan is to set right down and make two smoke fires, keep them a-going, holler every little while, and keep calm. Ye won't come to no harm unless ye'r a blame fool, an' such ought to stay to hum, where they'll be nursed.

Ernest Thompson Seton, *Two Little Savages,* 1904

In an emergency, it's important to stay calm and use as many signaling devices as possible to attract attention and help. These can range from a signal fire to mirrors, whistles, flashlights and flares. To signal SOS, use three short bursts of light or sound, followed by a pause, then three longer bursts, followed by a pause, then three short bursts (... _ _ _ ...). A smoke signal is made by allowing the fire to die down to hot coals and then adding green pine boughs or wet vegetation. Ground-to-air signals can be made in open spots with rocks and logs or drawn in the sand. An X indicates "unable to travel," an I "need doctor —emergency," an F "need food, water," an N "No" and a Y "Yes."

The lines making these letters should be at least 3 feet (0.9 m) wide. Waving brightly colored clothing on a branch can also alert pilots to campers in trouble.

Bibliography

Frazers [Fraser] River ... was never wholly passed by water before, and in all probability never will again ... and altho we ran all the rapids in safety, being perfectly light and having three of the most skilful Bowsmen in the country ... I should consider the passage down to be certain Death, in nine attempts out of Ten. I shall therefore no longer talk of it as a navigable stream.

George Simpson, running the Fraser River near Quesnel, British Columbia, 1828

Anderson, Scott. *Distant Fires*. Duluth, MN: Pfeifer-Hamilton, 1990.

Anderson, Thomas G. "Personal Narrative." Wisconsin Historical Collections, 1882.

Backes, David. *Canoe Country: An Embattled Wilderness*. Minocqua, Wisconsin: NorthWord Press, 1991.

Ballantyne, R. M. *Hudson Bay*. London: T. Nelson, 1879.

Cameron, Agnes Deans. *The New North: An Account of a Woman's 1908 Journey Through Canada to the Arctic*, ed. David Richeson. Saskatoon, Sask.: Western Producer Prairie Books, 1986.

Caras, Roger A. *Dangerous to Man: A Definitive Story of Wildlife's Reputed Dangers*. New York: Holt, Rinehart & Winston, 1975.

Davidson, James West, and John Rugge. *Great Heart: The History of a Labrador Adventure*. New York: Penguin Books, 1989.

_____. *The Complete Wilderness Paddler*. New York: Vintage Books, 1983.

Dowd, John. *Sea Kayaking: A Manual for Long-Distance Touring*. Vancouver: Douglas & McIntyre, 1988.

Dufresne, Jaclin. "Outdoor Stories (and Images)". http://www.jxd.qc.ca.

Fears, J. Wayne. *Complete Book of Outdoor Survival*. New York: Outdoor Life Books, 1986.

Ferguson, Paul. "Canoeing Labrador's Notakwanon River," in *Coastal CaNews* newsletter. http://www.comet.net/clubs/canoe/9610

Foster, John and Janet. *Adventures in Wild Canada.* Toronto: McClelland and Stewart, 1984.

Franks, C. E. S. *The Canoe and White Water.* Toronto: University of Toronto Press, 1977.

Friends of Quetico Park. *Pages from the Past: Voyageurs and Early Explorers.* Atikokan, ON: Friends of Quetico Park, 1992.

Hood, Robert. *To the Arctic by Canoe 1819-1821: The Journal and Paintings of Robert Hood, Midshipman with Franklin.*, ed. by C. Stuart Houston. Montreal: McGill-Queen's University Press, 1974.

Isaac, Jeff, and Peter Goth. *The Outward Bound Wilderness First-Aid Handbook.* Vancouver: Douglas & McIntyre, 1991.

Jason, Victoria. *Kabloona in the Yellow Kayak: One Woman's Journey Through the Northwest Passage.* Winnipeg: Turnstone Press, 1995.

Keighley, Sydney Augustus. *Trader, Tripper, Trapper.* Winnipeg: Watson & Dwyer Publishing, date unknown.

Koester, Robert J. ed. *Outdoor First-Aid.* Charlottesville, VA: dbS Productions, 1992.

Kopper, Philip. *The Wild Edge: Life and Lore of the Great Atlantic Beaches.* New York: Penguin, 1981.

Landry, Paul, and Matty McNair. *The Outward Bound Canoeing Handbook.* Vancouver: Douglas & McIntyre, 1992.

Leopold, Aldo. *A Sand County Almanac.* New York: Ballantine Books, 1970.

Lexicographical Centre for Canadian English. *A Concise Dictionary of Canadianisms.* Toronto: Gage Educational Publishing, 1973.

Mason, Bill. *Path of the Paddle: An Illustrated Guide to the Art of Canoeing.* Toronto: Key Porter Books, 1984.

_____. *Song of the Paddle: An Illustrated Guide to Wilderness Camping.* Toronto: Key Porter Books, 1988.

McDonald, Archibald. *Peace River: A Canoe Voyage from Hudson's Bay to the Pacific.* Edmonton: Hurtig, 1971.

McGuffin, Gary and Joanie. *Where Rivers Run: A 6,000-Mile Exploration of Canada by Canoe.* Toronto: Stoddart, 1988.

Morse, Eric W. *Freshwater Saga: Memoirs of a Lifetime of Wilderness Canoeing in Canada.* Toronto: University of Toronto Press, 1987.

88 BIBLIOGRAPHY

_____. *Fur Trade Canoe Routes of Canada/Then and Now*. Ottawa: National and Historic Parks Branch, 1969.

Murray, William H.H. *Adventures in the Wilderness*. Syracuse: Adirondack Museum/Syracuse University Press, 1989.

Nute, Grace Lee. *The Voyageur*. St. Paul: Minnesota Historical Society, 1987.

Olson, Sigurd. *The Singing Wilderness*. New York: Alfred A. Knopf, 1970.

_____. *The Lonely Land*. Toronto: McClelland & Stewart, 1972.

Patterson, R. M. *Far Pastures*. Sidney, B.C.: Gray's, 1963.

Phillips, David. *The Day Niagara Falls Ran Dry! Canadian Weather Facts and Trivia*. Toronto: Key Porter Books, 1993.

Revell, E. J. *'And Some Brought Flowers': Plants in a New World*. Toronto: University of Toronto Press, 1980.

Roberts, Kenneth G., and Philip Shackleton. *The Canoe: A History of the Craft from Panama to the Arctic*. Toronto: Macmillan, 1983.

Saunders, Audrey. *Algonquin Story*. Toronto: Department of Lands and Forests, 1963.

Seton, Ernest Thompson. *Two Little Savages*. London: Archibald Constable, 1904.

Sevareid, Eric. *Canoeing with the Cree*. St. Paul: Minnesota Historical Society, 1968.

Simpson, Sir George. *Fur Trade and Empire: George Simpson's Journal 1824-25*. Cambridge: Belknap Press of Harvard University Press, 1968.

Earl of Southesk, *Saskatchewan and the Rocky Mountains: A Diary and Narrative of Travel ... in 1859 and 1860*.

Washburne, Randel. *The Coastal Kayaker's Manual*. 2d edition. Old Saybrook, CT: The Globe Pequot Press, 1993.

There were some lively bits of river in that forty miles [Ghost Dam to Calgary], and on them the canoe also seemed to come alive. One could come down a riffle — which is a chute through or around a shingle bar — and drive the canoe close alongside the big waves; or through them, riding wildly on the crest of the mane. On rare occasions, I would meet a Canadian Pacific passenger train crawling slowly up into the hills. Nobody ever used that river; and the unexpected sight of a canoe never failed to cause a furore on board the train.... That was the time to give them their money's worth — and an extra drive on the paddle would lift the fore end of the canoe far out of the water as it leapt over some big wave.... Quite apart from the fun of showing off, there is a thrill about that which I have only found equalled when riding a fast horse and trying to corral a bunch of wild and obstreperous horses.

R. M. Patterson, running the Bow River, Alberta, 1930s

Trip Journal

My health being at length re-established and my wound healed ... I accordingly commenced a regular diary ... I at length succeeded in obtaining a very tolerable ink, by boiling the juice of the black-berry with a mixture of finely powdered charcoal and filtering it through a cloth ... As for quills I found no difficulty in procuring them, whenever I wanted, from the crows and ravens with which the beach was almost always covered, attracted by the offal of whales, seals &c ... while a large clam shell furnished me with an ink stand.

John R. Jewitt, *Narrative of the Adventures and Sufferings of John R. Jewitt, Only Survivor of the crew of the ship Boston,* 1807

100 Trip Journal

PETER MAHER built his first canvas canoe when he was fifteen years old in England, where he paddled on the Thames, the Wye and the Severn. Since moving to Toronto in 1965 to pursue an award-winning career as a designer, he has canoed or rafted on many of Canada's rivers, including the French, the Mattawa, the Magnetawan and the Tatshensheni. While living in France, he canoed the Nive, the Adour and the Tarn. Peter is also an avid hiker.

LAURIE COULTER, a Toronto writer and editor, began messing around in boats at her family's cottage in the Haliburton Highlands of Ontario. The first boats she owned were a kayak and a small sailboat, both built by her father. Her enthusiasm for canoe trips was sparked by working as an editor with some of Canada's best-known wilderness explorers, including Bill Mason and John and Janet Foster.

Peter and Laurie are partners with Paula Chabanais in Russet Books, the creators of *Cottages, Cabins & Chalets: An Owner's Guide for Guests*, published by Doubleday Canada Limited.

143 Trip Journal